Pagan P
&
Shaman Pa

...an ever-growing library of shared knowledge.

Moon Books has created two unique series where leading authors and practitioners come together to share their knowledge, passion and expertise across the complete Pagan spectrum. If you would like to contribute to either series, our proposal procedure is simple and quick, just visit our website (www.MoonBooks.net) and click on Author Inquiry to begin the process.

If you are a reader with a comment about a book or a suggestion for a title we'd love to hear from you! You can find us at facebook.com/MoonBooks or you can keep up to date with new releases etc on our dedicated Portals page at facebook.com/ paganportalsandshamanpathways/

'Moon Books has achieved that rare feat of being synonymous with top-quality authorship AND being endlessly innovative and exciting.'
Kate Large, Pagan Dawn

Pagan Portals

Animal Magic, Rachel Patterson
An introduction to the world of animal magic and working with animal spirit guides

Australian Druidry, Julie Brett
Connect with the magic of the southern land, its seasons, animals, plants and spirits

Blacksmith Gods, Pete Jennings
Exploring dark folk tales and customs alongside the magic and myths of the blacksmith Gods through time and place

Brigid, Morgan Daimler
Meeting the Celtic Goddess of Poetry, Forge, and Healing Well

By Spellbook & Candle, Mélusine Draco
Why go to the bother of cursing, when a bottling or binding can be just as effective?

By Wolfsbane & Mandrake Root, Mélusine Draco
A study of poisonous plants, many of which have beneficial uses in both domestic medicine and magic

Candle Magic, Lucya Starza
Using candles in simple spells, seasonal rituals and essential craft techniques

Celtic Witchcraft, Mabh Savage
Wield winds of wyrd, dive into pools of wisdom; walk side by side with the Tuatha Dé Danann

Dancing with Nemetona, Joanna van der Hoeven
An in-depth look at a little-known Goddess who can help bring peace and sanctuary into your life

Fairy Witchcraft, Morgan Daimler
A guidebook for those seeking a path that combines modern Neopagan witchcraft with the older Celtic Fairy Faith

God-Speaking, Judith O'Grady
What can we do to save the planet? Three Rs are not enough. Reduce, reuse, recycle...and religion

Gods and Goddesses of Ireland,
Meet the Gods and Goddesses of Pagan Ireland in myth and modern practice

Grimalkyn: The Witch's Cat, Martha Gray
A mystical insight into the cat as a power animal

Hedge Riding, Harmonia Saille
The hedge is the symbolic boundary between the two worlds and this book will teach you how to cross that hedge

Hedge Witchcraft, Harmonia Saille
Learning by experiencing is about trusting your instincts and connecting with your inner spirit

Hekate, Vivienne Moss
The Goddess of Witches, Queen of Shades and Shadows, and the ever-eternal Dark Muse haunts the pages of this poetic devotional, enchanting those who love Her with the charm only this Dark Goddess can bring

Runes, Kylie Holmes
The Runes are a set of 24 symbols that are steeped in history, myths and legends. This book offers practical and accessible information for anyone to understand this ancient form of divination

Sacred Sex and Magick, Web PATH Center
Wrap up ecstasy in love to create powerful magick, spells and healing

Spirituality without Structure, Nimue Brown
The only meaningful spiritual journey is the one you consciously undertake

The Awen Alone, Joanna van der Hoeven
An introductory guide for the solitary Druid

The Cailleach, Rachel Patterson
Goddess of the ancestors, wisdom that comes with age, the weather, time, shape-shifting and winter

The Morrigan, Morgan Daimler
On shadowed wings and in raven's call, meet the ancient Irish Goddess of war, battle, prophecy, death, sovereignty, and magic

Urban Ovate, Brendan Howlin
Simple, accessible techniques to bring Druidry to the wider public

Your Faery Magic, Halo Quin
Tap into your Natural Magic and become the Fey you are

Zen Druidry, Joanna van der Hoeven
Zen teachings and Druidry combine to create a peaceful life path
that is completely dedicated to the here and now

Shaman Pathways

Aubry's Dog, Melusine Draco
A practical and essential guide to using canine magical energies

Black Horse White Horse, Mélusine Draco
Feel the power and freedom as Black Horse, White Horse guides
you down the magical path of this most noble animal

Celtic Chakras, Elen Sentier
Tread the British native shaman's path, explore the Goddess
hidden in the ancient stories; walk the Celtic chakra spiral
labyrinth

Druid Shaman, Danu Forest
A practical guide to Celtic shamanism with exercises and
techniques as well as traditional lore for exploring the Celtic
Otherworld

Elen of the Ways, Elen Sentier
British shamanism has largely been forgotten: the reindeer
Goddess of the ancient Boreal forest is shrouded in mystery...
follow her deer-trods to rediscover her old ways

Following the Deer Trods, Elen Sentier
A practical handbook for anyone wanting to begin the old British
paths. Follows on from Elen of the Ways

Trees of the Goddess, Elen Sentier
Work with the trees of the Goddess and the old ways of Britain

Way of the Faery Shaman, Flavia Kate Peters
Your practical insight into Faeries and the elements they engage
to unlock real magic that is waiting to help you

Web of Life, Yvonne Ryves
A new approach to using ancient ways in these contemporary
and often challenging times to weave your life path

What people are saying about

GWYN AP NUDD

Gwyn ap Nudd was figuratively and literally lost to the mists of time (his name means "Light, son of Mist"). But now Danu Forest has brought the lore and his stories back out into the world, retrieving it from where it lay in the shadow of the Otherworld. In this book, we learn the tales of Gwyn, alongside his queen and his competitor, presented beautifully with exercises and practical advice for the seeker. Having just begun my quest to develop relationship with Gwyn ap Nudd, this book was a treasure trove of information, well-researched and brilliantly executed. Danu's skill with words and presentation of the material shines through all of her work, this book included. Her passion and work in the world is evident throughout, and inspires us on our own paths as we seek out the Old Ways, the the gods and goddesses, the songs of the land and the awen within our own hearts.

Joanna van der Hoeven, author of the best-selling *The Awen Alone: Walking the Path of the Solitary Druid* and *The Crane Bag: A Druid's Guide to Ritual Tools and Practices*. www.joannavanderhoeven.com

Pagan Portals: Gwyn ap Nudd is a fascinating and much needed look at this God. Balancing myth and modern practice, folk-lore and personal experience this short book is the perfect introduction to the Welsh leader of the Wild Hunt and King of Annwfn. A wonderful addition to any seeker's library and essential reading for anyone interested in the Welsh pantheon or fairylore.

Morgan Daimler, author of *Fairycraft and Fairies: A Guide to the Celtic Fair Folk*

Danu Forest eloquently places the shadowy figure of Gwyn on the secure foundation which he deserves – the ancient myths of Britain,

Wales and Ireland – enabling him to take his place as the psycho-pomp (soul guide) between the worlds.

Nicholas R. Mann, author of *The Isle of Avalon* and *Druid Magic*

Pagan Portals

GWYN AP NUDD

WILD GOD OF FAERY

GUARDIAN OF ANNWN

Pagan Portals

GWYN AP NUDD

WILD GOD OF FAERY

GUARDIAN OF ANNWN

Danu Forest

MOON
BOOKS

Winchester, UK
Washington, USA

JOHN HUNT PUBLISHING

First published by Moon Books, 2018
Moon Books is an imprint of John Hunt Publishing Ltd., No. 3 East Street, Alresford
Hampshire SO24 9EE, UK
office@jhpbooks.com
www.johnhuntpublishing.com
www.moon-books.net

For distributor details and how to order please visit the 'Ordering' section on our website.

ISBN: 978 1 78535 629 2
978 1 78535 630 8 (ebook)
Library of Congress Control Number: 2017949637

A CIP catalogue record for this book is available from the British Library.

Design: Stuart Davies

UK: Printed and bound by CPI Group (UK) Ltd, Croydon, CR0 4YY
US: Printed and bound by Thomson-Shore, 7300 West Joy Road, Dexter, MI 48130

We operate a distinctive and ethical publishing philosophy in
all areas of our business, from our global network of authors to
production and worldwide distribution.

Contents

For my son

With heartfelt thanks to the Old Gods, to the spirits of the Awen and to Dan Goodfellow (dangoodfellow.co.uk) for his endless support and beautiful illustrations. With thanks to the Glastonbury White Spring, and to Dr Gwilym Morus-Baird (welshmythology. com) for his support with my research. Thanks also to the Grove of the Avalon Sidhe, Nicholas R. Mann, and all those others who have inspired me and whose knowledge has guided me along the way, without whom this work would ever have been completed.

INTRODUCTION

I would shelter you and keep you in light,
But I can only teach you night vision.
Suzanne Vega

My first encounters with Gwyn ap Nudd began long ago, before I ever realised it was his presence that I felt, deep in the forest under a full moon. Something, a call, a tug at my spirit which I felt was impossible to ignore lead me irresistibly into a greater and greater closeness with the land that bore me, and to allow the process to provide its own initiations upon my soul. A witch, a druid, a *banfháidh,* and an *awenydd* at heart, I was always attracted to notions of the wild man of the woods, and the faery folk, the shining ones within the hollow hills ... following the footprints of my ancestors and their lingering traces upon the land lead me to seek the wild places in the world, finding treasure and deep magic in the shadows and in-between spaces. Gwyn became known to me as both a guide and a guardian of this path, protector of the land and its sacred inner realm.

Gwyn is known in Glastonbury where I live as a local hunter god, and king of the Faeries, dwelling in the mythological glass castle within Glastonbury Tor, a great hill that rises above the Avalon marshes in Somerset and can be seen for miles. A liminal place often shrouded in mist during the winter months it is a place that lends itself easily to thoughts of the Otherworld even in modern times, when an interest in Gwyn has been revived along with the indigenous myths and spiritual practices of which he is one of our main, if long forgotten, gods. At the foot of the Tor sits the famous Chalice Well and its red iron-rich waters, and the White Spring – an endless source of calcium-rich water that gushes almost endlessly from within the hill, which is now housed in a water temple that was once an old pump house. These two

1

waters, the red and the white have been held sacred for millennia and represent the duality of life, the male and female, life and death, blood and semen, and of course the red and white dragons of British myth. It was here, in the White Spring, where I was, as his dedicated priestess, first asked to set up a small public shrine to Gwyn many years ago, after holding a series of public ceremonies there dedicated to him and the ancient British tradition. I was perhaps the first to honour him with a public shrine and open ceremonies for hundreds of years. Each Nos Calan Gaeaf/Samhain (Oct 31st) and Calan Mai/Beltane (1st May), I now lead an ever-growing number of people all around the world honouring Gwyn as lord of Annwfn and guardian of the land, as well as the king of faerie, those mysterious beings who live closer to the soul of the land herself than we can imagine.

Gwyn ap Nudd offers each their own initiations, their own lessons to know not only Annwfn, the soul of the land, but also to know themselves. A spiritual journey without end, Gwyn teaches us something of the shadow so that we may find the light within ourselves. Our own myths and wounded places function as offerings for growth and healing, whereby bit by bit, we may become like the poet Taliesin, radiant and illuminated from within, worthy to encounter the great cauldron, the great goddess of the land herself, and become renewed in her depths. He also shows us how magical and blessed and luminous the world can be, when we are filled to the brim with the cauldrons brew, the precious Awen, the inspiration of the spirit.

There are many continuous threads that appear time and again for those who work with Gwyn, many lessons and themes that he presents to each of us about challenging or acknowledging the parts of us that we ignore or supress, whether that be by courage or compassion. Just as he leads the dead in the Wild Hunt, he guides us to let go of those things within us that no longer serve us, and encourages us to cross over into a greater sense of life and death than we held before. Together with an exploration of the remaining literary sources we have for how our ancestors honoured Gwyn, and developing an ever-closer connection with the landscape upon which they lived, these provide a strong body of lore and practice for helping us to re-remember this ancient Brythonic god and connect, each in our own way, no matter where or how we live, coming to the path just as we are.

In this book, we will be exploring Gwyn ap Nudd through his various forms and tales, from King of the faeries, and lord of the forest, to guardian of the underworld and leader of the dead, and seeking ways to walk with our own darkness on the quest for our own Awen, our souls and our own self-knowledge, diving into the depths and drinking from the great cauldron until we arise at last reborn and radiant, filled with the light within the land.

This small book is an offering to Gwyn ap Nudd, in service and with gratitude.

DF 2017 Glastonbury.

Chapter 1

GWYN AP NUÐÐ – WHITE SON OF MIST

The heathy headland of the family of Gwyn
It is often speckled smoke:
The rising vapour which surrounds the woods of May.
Unsightly fog wherein the dogs are barking,
Ointment of the witches of Annwfn.
Dafydd ap Gwilym 'The Mist'/'Y Niwl' (fourteenth century)

Gwyn ap Nudd, guardian of Annwfn the Brythonic underworld and king of the Tylwyth Teg, the Welsh faeries, has long captured the imagination of poets and artists, from the ancient bardic tradition to modern-day fantasy writers. An ancient god of the Britons he has none the less survived the Christian period as a figure of both fear and longing, as a keeper of demons when the pagan Annwfn was transformed in the popular imagination into the Christian hell – and as a figure of romance and faery glamour; a courtly ruler within his glass castle, a handsome faery lover with his many courts within the hollow hills and barrow mounds of Wales and Western England, a horned warrior god, antler crowned, fierce spirit of the wild, and Winter king, *the Brenin Llwyd – the grey king in the mist –* aloof and unknowable. Accompanied by his faery hounds the *Cŵn Annwfn* he leads the dead to the realms beyond as lord of the wild hunt, soaring over the wild Welsh hills on faery rades (rides) with storm clouds in his wake, and as guardian of Annwfn he facilitates our transformation after death as we return once more to the great cauldron within the land. As faery lord of the forest, he is found in the wild places and on the hills and mountains, cloaking them with mist ... tempting lovers and inspiring bards and visionaries who to this day will

4

seek out solitary retreat in such places to undergo his initiations of the spirit, to return *dead, mad ... or a poet.*

The name *Gwyn* is traditionally translated as 'White', 'Fair', 'Holy' or 'Blessed'. Throughout the Celtic traditions we see the motif of something intrinsically good or spiritually enlightened being connected to the colour white, or literally emitting light or shining in some way. We could see this as describing someone as illuminated or radiant with some inner divine light or wisdom. This can be seen with the old Irish gods, the Tuatha de Danann, often called the 'Shining Ones', and their later forms as beings of Faery or the Sidhe, are also described as luminescent in some way, implying a state of blessedness, radiating the light within the land. Gwyn's Irish counterpart is Fionn Mac Cumhail, who also means 'Fair', and who was spiritually illuminated by the *Imbas* – which equates with the Welsh *Awen* – poetic or oracular inspiration, and given magical powers of divination after consuming the salmon of knowledge. The Welsh Gwyn can be translated directly as *Fionn* in Gaelic, *Find* in Old Irish and *Vindo* in Gaulish, and has its roots the Proto-Indo-European *'weid'* "to see, to know". It shares this linguistic root with the word druid, who has the knowledge, or the vision, of the *dru* – the oak. 'Weid' is also the root of our English word *wisdom*.

The roots of Gwyn and Fionn lie in an early Celtic god Vindonnus – usually taken to mean 'white' or 'clear light'. Vindonnus is usually taken to be a Gaulish aspect of the god Apollo, worshipped most notably in Burgundy, eastern France where a healing spring was dedicated to him. Apollo was both a Greek and Roman god and one with a complex set of attributes covering healing, prophecy, the poetic arts and music, as well as the sun and the light. His worship was widespread and he was particularly associated with oracles, his most famous being that at Delphi. Apollo was usually considered to be the Classical/Romano version of the Celtic god Belenus 'fair shining one', who is associated like Apollo with the sun, but also with fire, as patron god of the Celtic festival every May 1st – Beltane 'the bright fire'. Some scholars cast doubt on Belenus' and Apollo's roles as sun gods, as their roles separate over time from purely solar functions, but as the overseer of Beltane, Belenus is not only a solar god, but one who oversees a rise in life force and fertility. His 'bright fire' has as much to do with healing – traditionally the fires were used as much to banish illness as they were to celebrate a rise in vitality and fertility generally, and the light that he brings may equally be an inner illumination or surge in well-being. Academics consider Belenus Vindonnus to be especially concerned with healing eyes as many offerings found at his spring represented eyes, but the white or clear light he embodies could also be this inner illumination or inner vision, clear sight metaphorically as well as literally.

Ap or its earlier form *Map*, literally means *son* or *son of* and is cognate with the Scots Gaelic *Mac*.

Nudd (pronounced neeth) means *mist* in Welsh, but is also another name for a legendary Welsh hero Lludd LLaw Erient, *Lludd* or *Nudd of the Silver hand*. Nudd/Lludd was mentioned in the Welsh Triads as one of the three most generous men in Wales. However, his name also connects him to the Irish divine king Nuada, or Nuadu Airgetlám – *'Nuada of the silver hand'*. Many early Welsh genealogies treat Nudd as an historical figure, but he is most likely derived from the early British god Nodens, whose worship appears to have similarities with or is the Brythonic equivalent of Nuada. His temple near Lydney, Gloucestershire suggests he was a god of healing and dream incubation, with connections to hunting and the sea. Those in need of healing or advice would make prayers and offer gifts to the god, before sleeping in special cubicles in the temple, in the hope of an oracular healing dream.

We can imagine Nudd/Nuada then to be a god of mist and cloud, but it seems unlikely that this is merely a god of misty or cloudy weather. Mist and fog are powerful symbols of transition and liminality in much Celtic literature, the legendary mists surrounding the Isle of Avalon being a prime example. To embark on any spiritual or healing journey we must encounter these liminal spaces, where the solid earth seems to melt and become indistinct, where our senses, our vision and direction may be clouded and confused for a while, where we must step forward bravely, trusting in our destination and our inner navigation to guide us. When we consider Nodens, this idea of liminality gains more traction in relation to healing dreams and sleep, where some sort of journey into the Other – or Inner worlds takes place. We get the sense that this is someone to do with a healing inner journey, changes of consciousness and seeking vision, wisdom and renewal, the Awen which may then be carried up into the everyday, waking world.

The name Nodens may come from several places, all of which are illuminating in connection with this discussion. The most popular root for the word amongst academics is probably the Celtic stem *noudont* or *noudent*, meaning to acquire, or have the use of, and earlier to catch or trap, as a hunter or fisherman, from the Proto-Indo-European *neu-d* meaning to acquire, or fish. At Lydney there were several statues of hunting dogs, which are traditionally connected with healing, but also to the gods of the hunt and the forest. There were also other artefacts such as bronze reliefs depicting a sea deity, fishermen and tritons. Perhaps it was believed that a healing sleep was a way to hunt a cure from across the waters of consciousness, or to fish one up from the depths of the Otherworld. Another suggestion has been that the name Nodens come from the Proto-Celtic *sNowdo* or *sNoudo* meaning mist or clouds, the 'sN' being changed to N in the P-Celtic languages of Gaulish and Brythonic. This idea hits a problem with the fact that the sN still occurs in Old Irish which would therefore make it *Snuada* rather than *Nuada*. However, language is always a fluid thing over such large spans of time so there is still some potential for this argument and it is entirely possible the names Nudd, Nuada and Nodens developed from a combination of these roots. Nudd / Nuada/ Nodens might then be understood as some kind of hunter

7

deity, a trapper of prey even, in the mist. We know him from his tales and his temple that he was a deity the sick or troubled came to for help, therefore we know he is a beneficent god, so a guide or ally perhaps in uncertain realms, in search perhaps of Gwyn, the illumination, the blessing, the inner radiance of the soul and healing remedy.

Practice: Seeking Gwyn ap Nudd

Seek out Gwyn whenever the wind blows; for in oral tales they say he and his people come on the wind … seek him when you see the mist gathering on the hills and valleys, at dusk or dawn, the thin doorways of the day between the realms above the realm within. Seek him in the reflections of starlight upon deep still water, and when you hear an owl screech in the night, or see the geese fly overhead on winter evenings … know that he is close. Close your eyes and feel the air on your skin, the promise of things unseen just a breath away.

Wander into the wild, the edges of the waters, the green and hidden places and the high hills. Find your voice in the still places when you are alone, and give him gifts of song and poetry, gifts of remembered tales and twining rhyme, carrying your heart with them – uttered in a whisper on the breeze or a shout upon the storm. Give him the truth of you, share with him your fierce spirit and your tears and know no shame, for at the end of it all when you time is done he will come for you still, better as a friend than a stranger.

Practice: Entering the Forest

Awenyddion- those inspired by the Awen, bards and wise women would always honour the spirits and seek permission when entering the wild places on the land for wisdom and communion. A traditional prayer to Gwyn at such times was this:

ad regem Eumenidium et reginam eius: Gwynn ap Nwdd qui es ultra in silvis pro amore concubine tue permitte nos venire domum (14th Century.)

To the King of the Spirits and his queen: Gwyn ap Nudd, you who are yonder in the forest, for the love of your mate, permit me to enter your dwelling.[1]

Go to the wild places, go to the places where the deep green of trees and the rushing rivers surround you and the modern world is held at bay. Let nature be your greatest guide when seeking the old gods, especially Gwyn. When you get out into nature of any kind, try this exercise:

Close your eyes and take three steadying deep breaths. Try to quiet your mind as much as possible and just listen. What can you hear? Are there birds in the trees? Insects? A breeze ruffling the leaves? Try for a moment to open your heart up to the spirit of this place, its essence and atmosphere, try to sense it as a living being in its own right.

Now call out to Gwyn as Lord of the Forest, in your own way, or you may like to use these traditional words quoted above.

Tune in to your heart and the feeling in your belly – do you feel you are welcome to proceed? You may be fortunate enough to hear or see Gwyn's reply, in a flash of vision or a single word in your ear perhaps – but more often than not it is tuning in to these finer senses within us that can teach us the most – where our brain cannot interfere. How do you feel?

If you feel you can proceed, focus a moment on your feet and the ground beneath you, the path stretching ahead of you through the trees. Now slowly put one foot in front of the other and walk along the path, calm and present to this sacred place where the worlds meet.

Breathe in the air – what can you smell? The green forest smell of leaves and rich earth? The dank but good smell of leaf mould? As you walk, call up the energy from the land, let every footfall be a prayer to call it in, to connect with its unique spirit and breathe it into your being. With each step fill yourself with the wild green energy of the forest.

Let your feet lead you, finding your way through the trees until you come to a place that feels as if it has a special atmosphere. It may be a large ancient tree, an open clearing, a burrow opening or the bowl-shaped shelter formed by an uprooted tree, the roots torn from the earth making a thick wall around you. When you find a place that seems to have a special resonance, sit down and make yourself comfortable, let your bones and muscles relax into the earth, into the wood and stone.

Continue to breathe in the energy of the forest, of the green world, and gently extend your senses all around you; the branches overhead, the roots below. Try to sense all the life that surrounds you. With every out breath stretch out your connection, and with every in breath breathe in more of the life force that surrounds you.

As you look around you, hold in your awareness that you are surrounded by spirits, that every tree, plant, insect, animal, fungi, breath of wind, drop of rain, cloud overhead is a sentient being, a spirit, a soul in its own right.

Here you will find, if you are patient, the secret ones, the Tylwyth Teg, the faery folk and the Lord of the forest himself, but give it time, and return often. Let the magic of the forest seep into your heart and soul.

Chapter 2

ANNUFN ANÒ ThE REALM OF FAERY

Twrch Trwyth will not be hunted until Gwyn son of Nudd is found –
God has put the spirit of the demons of Annwfn in him, lest the world
be destroyed. He will not be spared from there[2]

Annwn, (pronounced Anoon) or in its earlier form, *Annwfn*
(Anooven) means 'the deep place' and is the Welsh name for the
spirit realm or the underworld, over which Gwyn is traditionally
held to be guardian and lord. Over the Christian era this became
understood as a Welsh version of hell. According to this quote
above from *The Tale of Culhwch and Olwen*, (from the collection
of Welsh traditional tales, the Mabinogion and first recorded in
the White Book of Rhydderch circa 1325) we can see that even in
this later Christian era Gwyn is given a high status, and must be
considered to be a figure of great goodness and power, even if with
a somewhat terrifying reputation as he is tasked with the restraint
of all the 'demons' of Annwfn, 'lest the world be destroyed'. In a
Gaulish curse tablet there is a reference to *antumnos* which may
have the same root as *Annwfn* and comes from the Gallo-Brittonic
word *ande-dubnos* meaning the underworld, the dark place. Yet
the Welsh underworld, and indeed the underworld in the Celtic
tradition generally was not a place of darkness or judgement as
it's commonly understood in a monotheistic world view. Rather
it is a place of paradisal delight and beauty – of ease and deep
soul connection with the land and its spirit inhabitants, the faeries,
together with the gods. When we consider the name 'the deep
place' a whole host of connotations arise, that not only a place
deep underground or below water is referred to, but perhaps also
somewhere deep inside reality as well as deep inside the human

heart itself.

Annwfn often reflects the surface world. There are tales that suggest a form of learning takes place for those who come there, as well as an opportunity for healing and rest – it seems to be a place where the soul can re-set itself after the trials and woes of the mortal world, where some reconnection can take place with the inner vivifying qualities of the land.

Annwfn, like other Celtic forms of the underworld or Otherworld can be accessed via visionary or physical journeys into the earth itself, via barrow mounds and hollow hills, but it can also be discovered under lakes or across the sea much like the Irish Otherworlds of *Tir Na NÓg* – 'the land of the ever young' or *Tir Tairngire* 'the land of promise'. Annwfn like the other Celtic spirit realms can also be entered quite by mistake or of a sudden while living in the mortal world, when the two seem to blur into one another and suddenly the hero of the tale has crossed over into something else entirely; the shift first becoming apparent by encountering one of its inhabitants – such as in the tale of Pwyll encountering the *Cŵn Annwfn*, the otherworldly hounds while out hunting, in the first branch of the Mabinogion. In this tale Annwfn can be found within the mortal Welsh realm of Dyfed, and in other parts of the Mabinogion, Annwfn can be found in the real-world locations of Harlech and on the island of Grassholm in Pembrokeshire, whereas in the Arthurian poem *Preiddeu Annwfn* or 'the spoils of Annwfn' by Taliesin, Annwfn is located on an island across the sea.

Preiddeu Annwfn/The spoils of Annwn[3]

I praise the lord, ruler of a king's realm
Who has extended his dominion over the shore of the world.
Well prepared was Gweir's prison in Caer Sidi
During the time of Pwyll and Pryderi.
No one went there before him.
The heavy blue grey chain held the faithful servant,

And before the spoils of Annwfn he sings in woe,
And our bardic invocation shall continue until doom.
Three times the fill of Prydwen we went into it;
Except seven, none returned from Caer Sidi.

I am fair in fame if my song is heard
In Caer Pedryfan, with its four sides revolving;
My poetry from the cauldron was uttered,
Ignited by the breath of nine maidens.
The cauldron of the chief of Annwfn, was sought
With its dark rim and pearls.
It does not boil the coward's portion, it is not its destiny.
A shining sword was thrust into it,
And it was left behind in Lleminog's hand.
And before the door of hell's gate, lamps burned.
And when we went with Arthur, glorious in misfortune,
Except seven, none returned from Caer Vedwyd.

I am fair in fame: my songs are heard
In Caer Pedryfan, Isle of the strong shining door
Fresh water and jet run together;
Bright wine their drink before their retinue.
Three times the fill of Prydwen we went by sea:
Except seven, none returned from Caer Rigor.

I set no value on insignificant men concerned with scripture,
They did not see the valour of Arthur beyond Caer Wydyr:
Six thousand men stood upon the wall.
It was hard to speak with their sentinel.
Three times the fill of Prydwen went with Arthur
Except seven, none returned from Caer Golud.

I set no value on insignificant men with their trailing robes
They do not know what was created on what day.

When at mid-day Cwy was born.
Or who made the one who did not go to the meadows of Defwy;
They do not know the Brindled ox or his yoke
With seven score links on his collar.
And when we went with Arthur, dolorous journey
Except seven none returned from Caer Vandwy.

I set no value on insignificant men with weak wills,
Who do not know on what day the chief was created,
When at mid-day the ruler was born,
What animal they keep with his silver head.
When we went with Arthur, piteous battle
Except seven none returned from Caer Ochren.

Congregating monks howl like a choir of dogs
From a clash with the lords who know
Whether the wind has one course, whether the sea is all one,
Whether the fire is all one spark of fierce tumult?

Monks congregate like wolves
From a clash with lords who know.
The monks do not know how the light and dark divide,
Nor the winds course, or the storm,
The place where it ravages, the place it strikes,
How many saints are in the Otherworld, how many on earth?
I praise the lord, the great chief:
May I not endure sadness: Christ will reward me.

This poem attributed to the bard Taliesin, and possibly written or at least composed as early as the eighth century CE, before finally being recorded in the fourteenth-century *Book of Taliesin*, recounts a raid on the underworld Annwfn by King Arthur in order, presumably, to steal the cauldron that resides there.

Many of the references in Preiddeu Annwfn are quite obscure, however, there are several aspects of the piece that relate to other remaining works and extend our knowledge of Annwfn. The raid itself is referred to as an aside in the Mabinogion tale of Culhwch and Olwen, where Arthur and his retinue sail across the sea to Ireland aboard his ship Prydwen to obtain the cauldron of Dirwrnach/Dyrnwch the Giant, which it was said would never boil the meat of a coward. Here the cauldron is seized and becomes one of the thirteen treasures of the Island of Britain although little more is known of it, including its location. In the poem, the raid is far less successful resulting in almost total death and destruction for Arthur and his men. A similar doomed voyage occurs when Bran the Blessed gives a life-restoring cauldron to his new brother-in-law Matholwch, but when Matholwch mistreats his sister Branwen, Bran is forced to rescue her and the cauldron is destroyed in the process. Just as in this poem, there are no survivors of the raid except seven men, including Taliesin and Pwyll and Rhiannon's son, Pryderi. Taliesin's connection to both tales and the same number of survivors show us this is the same tale recounted numerous times in different forms, and the cauldron itself is revealed very much as a central character in events rather than a mute object. Instead we may see that the Cauldron is in fact the sovereignty of the land, its heart and soul, the goddess incarnate, as embodied by Branwen, or Gwyn's queen, Creiddylad – as discussed later – and sought after by numerous mortal world and Otherworldly forces.

The main reference to the attempted theft of the cauldron occurs in stanza 2, lines 8-9. "A shining sword was thrust into it/ And it was left behind in Lleminog's hand" remains ambiguous. It is taken by some to mean that that cauldron was stolen, or even broken by Lleminog – whose name means *'leaping one'* and is potentially either an epithet for Arthur, or a reference to the Irish god Lugh. Lugh or Lugus is thought to be the god of oaths, his name meaning 'to swear an oath' although it is sometimes thought to also mean 'bright' and 'shining'. It may be that it was left in the hand of Lugh as a matter of oath, or judgement of an oath-breaking after the attempted raid, like one of its Irish counterparts, the four-sided cup of truth that shatters when a lie is spoken over it, and reforms when a truth is said over the pieces.

17

However, when we consider the line "A shining sword was thrust into it" we see another possible meaning arise – that of a moment of conception – albeit in dramatic and even violent imagery, resulting in the attainment of the cauldron by Lleminog even if somewhat briefly. Given that the raid is disastrous and none survive 'except seven' men it is far from given that they were successful in the theft, or even if that was the real aim. Although the theft is referred to in Culhwch and Olwen we must remember that the quest for the cauldron – for the soul and womb of the land – is a perennial quest of the spirit and not an historical account of a physical object. While the theme of its theft or shattering, like the loss of the grail, is a perennial symbol for the imperfect world and the wounded human condition, nonetheless it remains intact and whole for those who seek it in the heart of Annwfn itself – to either destroy or be renewed by, each in their turn and according to their nature.

Preiddeu Annwfn although Welsh in origin has much in common with the Irish Echtrai and later Immrama voyage tales which are of a similar age, and are also concerned with mortal adventures to Otherworldly destinations. Interestingly both the Lebor Gabála Érenn (The Book of the Taking of Ireland) which was compiled finally in the eleventh century and Nennius's Historia Brittonum (ninth century CE) both discuss the Milesians, the ancestors to the Irish, encountering a glass fortress in the sea. Just as in Preiddeu Annwfn the inhabitants will not talk with them "It was hard to speak with their sentinel." (stanza 5, line 4) and when the Milesians attack the majority of them are killed.

In the poem Preiddeu Annwfn, we see the otherworld of Annwfn given many titles, each describing its action or function, or perhaps even how Annwfn may be accessed. Let's work through it stage by stage.

1) Caer Sidi – the fortress of the sidhe, or faery. . Suggesting access to Annwfn may occur through encounters with faery. Transgressors or those chosen by the faeries and spirits may

become imprisoned there. *"well prepared was the prison of Gweir in Caer Sidi,"* (stanza 1, line 3) Equally the faithful servant may be the initiate undergoing a period of ritual constraint or time held in the Otherworld.

2) *"The heavy blue grey chain held the faithful servant,"* (stanza 1, line 6) We also see here that Annwfn is accessed by going across water or across the sea, a recurring motif across Celtic literature. Equally this may represent a shift in consciousness, or emotional state, in Jungian terms accessing the collective unconscious or the shamanic state where all things become one.

3) *"In Caer Pedryfan, with its four sides revolving,"* (stanza 2, line 2) here we see the four-sided castle, or the castle with four revolutions. This bears a resemblance to the tower at Harlech where Bran the Blessed's men were entertained by his head after his death, in a kind of mourning or holding zone. The four sides may refer to the four directions, or the turn of the seasonal wheel, suggesting perhaps that the task here is to gain knowledge of the seasons and the land on which you dwell in each direction until a sense of centredness and still presence is attained. Caer Pedryfan may also relate to the four-sided cup of truth, discussed above, which shatters if it hears a lie and comes together again when it hears a truth spoken over it.

4) *"The cauldron of the chief of Annwfn,"* (Stanza 2, line 5) Given further details in the poem, and surrounding lore we can see here that the chief of Annwn/Annwfn is in fact Gwyn, known here as Dyrnwch the Giant, just as he is known in the first branch of the Mabinogion as Arawn.

5) *"Except seven, none returned from Caer Vedwyd."* (stanza 2, line 12) Caer Vedwyd is usually translated as the castle or fortress of the mead feast, that is, of feasting and celebration. Here we see a reference to an altered state of consciousness brought on by drink or other substances.

6) *"Except seven, none returned from Caer Rigor,"* (stanza 3, line 6) The fortress of stiffness or rigidity. Sometimes interpreted as the

fortress of royalty though this is unlikely. The castle of rigor, as in rigor mortis, where the muscles in a dead body stiffen and become rigid. Here we see a reference to Annwfn as realm of the dead and the process of death and decay perhaps being an initiatory path after death, or re-enacted by the living via ritual burial or immersion in darkness, as is referred to in other works by Taliesin.

7) *"They did not see the valour of Arthur beyond Caer Wydyr,"* (stanza 4, line 2) Caer Wydyr, the glass castle, connected to Avalon and Glastonbury and the last destination of Arthur. The poem suggests that only in Caer Wydyr where the raid took place was it witnessed, but also that only at Caer Wydyr could such things be seen – such ambiguity and multiplicity of meaning is a common feature of Bardic material. Access to Annwfn and its wisdom via Caer Wydyr is perhaps accessed by observation of the stellar realm and perhaps also through scrying – literally looking through the glass.

8) *"Except seven, none returned from Caer Golud."* (stanza 4, line 6) The fortress or castle of impediment, here we see Annwfn once more associated with the realm of the dead and the physical restraint and containment of an initiate. Another translation of *Golud* in modern Welsh is riches – the wealthy castle, the castle of riches, the castle of treasure. Sometimes translated as the gloomy castle suggesting its position between the night and day – a place in eternal twilight, or accessed through those liminal times such as dawn and dusk, life and death, although this translation is less reliable.

9) *"Except seven, none returned from Caer Vandwy."* (stanza 5 line 8) The high fortress, the castle of the gods' peak. Access to Annwfn and its wisdom has traditionally been gained by time spent in lonely remote places, especially the tops of mountains, such as on Cader Idris. Caer Vandwy is the same as that mentioned in the dialogue of Gwyn ap Nudd and Gwyddno Garanhir – discussed later – where Gwyn saw battle and conflict, presumably on the defending side of this raid against Arthur and his men.

10) *"Except seven, none returned from Caer Ochren."* (stanza 6, line 6) translations of Ochren are scarce and debated, but leading contenders are angular, or enclosed, possibly or "castle of the angular or shelving sides" e.g., a terraced slope. Given Annwfn's position surrounded by water this could be a reference to the tide line, the liminal place between the land and the sea. Such places are always considered highly magical, allowing the seeker to slip through the veil, being neither this nor that. Alternatively, this could be a reference to a terraced hill fort, or other high hill such as the terraces on the sides of Glastonbury Tor. In this context, we are looking at accessing Annwfn via ancestral contact on the land or entrance into the faery hollow hills once again.

11) The poem ends with the poet criticizing the monks who have by the time of writing converted the population and largely forgotten the old gods and the vast bodies of lore attached to them, as well as basing their own knowledge on their superiors rather than feeling or experiencing their own faith, in direct comparison to the state of all knowing attained and displayed by the poet (Taliesin) himself. Despite this the poet hedges his bets and seems to reconcile himself to the new faith. *"I praise the lord, the great chief: May I not endure sadness: Christ will reward me"* (stanza 7, lines 11-12). It should be noted, however, that while the poet mentions Christ this once, the lord and chief referred to may just as easily be the chief of Annwfn as the Christian god.

In conclusion, we therefore know Annwfn by several names each providing clues to gain access to the otherworldly realm and a traditional initiatory path.

Caer Sidi – Castle of the Sidhe/faeries. By connection with Faery and the fair folk, and entering the Faery realm. Usually this is down to them approaching the seeker, but with time spent in nature and offerings made to befriend them, greater contact is always possible.

Caer Pedryfan – The revolving castle. By becoming mindful and still whilst observing at length the turn of the seasons. By becoming closer to nature.

Caer Vedwyd – Castle of the mead feast. By celebration and carousal, by the ingestion of consciousness-altering substances.

Caer Rigor – Castle of stiffness/rigidity. By death or attaining a period of death-like restraint and containment, such as ritual burial or enclosure in darkened spaces.

Caer Wydyr – Castle of glass. By extended periods of astrological and stellar study and meditation upon the stellar realm.

Caer Golud – Castle of impediment. By death and constraint – again either in the earth or sacred darkness. Also, possibly illness, grief, depression and mental illness.

Caer Vandwy – The high castle, castle of the mountain peak/gods' peak. By meditation and observance at high places, especially mountain tops, which was a traditional bardic initiation and practice, such as spending the night or a prolonged period on Cader Idris.

Caer Ochren – Castle of the angular or shelving sides. By working in inner vision on the tide line on the sea shore, or by entering the faery mounds and terraced ancestral hillforts.

Practice: Cauldron scrying

In this exercise, we will seek self-knowledge, and Awen – vision and inspiration from the great cauldron via scrying – a divination technique using water and, optionally, sacred herbs.

Seek out some fresh mugwort *Artemisia vulgaris* (a traditional druidic plant for scrying and seeking vision) if you can, to burn as an offering when dried. Alternatively, you may steep some in oil for one whole month from dark moon to dark moon, before straining and storing in a dark glass bottle. Use the oil to anoint your brow and add a few drops upon the water when seeking vision.

You may also wish to gather some pebbles of jet, as mentioned in *Preiddeu Annwfn* to place in the water to aid you. Jet is traditionally used to help heal grief, and to grant protection – both suitable properties for a sacred stone associated with Annwfn, and found in the waters which separate the worlds. "Fresh water and jet run together" (*Preiddeu Annwfn* stanza 3, line 3).

Wait for dusk or darkness, and take a traditional black iron cauldron, or a dark-coloured bowl and fill with fresh water – from a natural spring or river for preference although cold tap water will do. Place in it the jet stones if you have them, and/or 3 drops of oil.

Seat yourself somewhere quiet – at the edge of trees or by the fireside are good places between the worlds. Breathe slowly and sit quietly, gently resting your eyes upon the surface of the water, and softly, under your breath, ask the waters of the cauldron to grant you wisdom if it will. Then leaning forward over the surface of the water, breathe gently upon its surface before sitting back, still resting your eyes gently upon the water.

Wait, in quiet stillness, for the visions to appear, in your inner vision or before you, according to your own gifts and nature.

When you are finished thank the water and the spirit of the cauldron, and pour the water upon the land at the foot of a tree or some precious plant, to return to the earth.

The Tylwyth Teg

The Fairy Glen above Bettws y Coed is called in Welsh Ffos 'Noddyn, 'the Sink of the Abyss'; but Mr. Gethin Jones told me that it was also called Glyn y Tylwyth Teg, which is very probable, as some such a designation is required to account for the English name, the Fairy Glen.' People on the Capel Garmon side used to see the Tylwyth playing there, and descending into the Ffos or Glen gently and lightly without occasioning themselves the least harm. The Fairy Glen was, doubtless, supposed to contain an entrance to the world below. This reminds one of the name of the pretty hollow running inland from the railway station at Bangor. Why should it be called Nant Uffern, or 'The Hollow of Hell'? Can it be that there was a supposed entrance to the fairy world somewhere there? In any case, I am quite certain that Welsh place-names involve allusions to the fairies much oftener than has been hitherto supposed; and I should be inclined to cite, as a further example, Moel Eilio, or Moel Ellian, from the personal name Eilian, to be mentioned presently. Moel Eilian is a mountain under which the fairies were supposed to have great stores of treasure. But to return to Mr. Gethin Jones, I had almost forgotten that I have another instance of his in point. He showed me a passage in a paper which he wrote in Welsh some time ago on the antiquities of Yspyty Ifan. He says that where the Serw joins the Conwy there is a cave, to which tradition asserts that a harpist was once allured by the Tylwyth Teg. He was, of course, not seen afterwards, but the echo of the music made by him and them on their harps is still to be heard a little lower down, under the field called to this day Gweirglodd y Telynorion, 'The Harpers' Meadow'.

John Rhys Celtic Folklore – Welsh and Manx, (1901, pp. 205-6)

A generic name for Welsh faeries, the Tylwyth Teg of 'fair folk' are most often said to be under the rulership of Gwyn and to live in the lakes and mountains of Dyfed, but are also said to enjoy visiting the markets and fishing towns, and may appear much like humans other than perhaps an excessive love of music and dancing. In folklore, they are portrayed as keen on visiting farmers' wives and being friendly to the peasantry overall although they should always be treated with respect and care, leaving them offerings of milk, cheese or butter. The Tylwyth Teg were often said to sweep the hearth or do other small tasks about the home, and were keen on bringing luck and love to those they liked, although conversely, they were often accused of stealing children (this seems to be a later addition). Tales abound of them seen dancing upon the hillsides in great numbers. *'Their music exercised an uncanny fascination. They lured young people into their circles to join them in the dance, and it was a task both difficult and dangerous to rescue these from their enchantments.'*[4]

These Faeries are also said to be particularly fond of the hunt and ride on grey or white horses, in great processions rather like the Scottish Faery 'rades' or rides.

The Gwragedd Annwfn

The Gwragedd Annwfn, or 'the wives of Annwfn' are a race of female water spirits connected to rivers and lakes, especially in the mountainous regions of Wales, although tales of them can be found all over. They are said to live beneath the water, or access their kingdom by travelling through it, and all of them are under the rulership of Gwyn ap Nudd. Often, they are said to live in submerged towns whose ghostly faery bells can still be heard on calm days. One such is Crumlyn or Crymlyn Lake near Briton Ferry in Neath, which was once said to contain a large faery palace. Another is the famous Llyn Barfog in Snowdonia, where the Gwragedd Annwfn are said to have been seen many times, gathering at dusk to drive their milk-white cows to feast on the grass near the water *'Clad all in green, accompanied by their milk white hounds'.*[5] The wives of Annwfn are often associated with magical faery cattle which yield the most and the richest milk, and seem to bestow great abundance and fertility on the land on which they roam. Faery cattle are reminiscent of the old Celtic cow goddesses, such as the Irish Boann 'white cow' who is both the goddess of the river Boyne and the wife of Nechtan, another name for Nuada/Nodens/Nudd. Boann is associated with fertility and abundance, but also healing and spiritual mysteries and training. The Goddess Brigid is said to have been fed on the milk of faery cows, which bestowed upon her some of her powers, and is sometimes said to be the daughter of Boann for this reason.

The Gwragedd Annwfn also bestow healing magic with their presence, and one famous story centres upon Llyn y Fan Fach. In the twelfthcentury there was a family of renowned herbal physicians which traced their healing skills to their faery mother. Their father

Rhiwallon was said to have been a poor farmer who carried away one of the Gwragedd Annwfn that used to emerge from the lake whilst he was grazing his flocks. The faery woman consented to marry him, so long as he should never strike her more than three times in all their years together. She brought with her seven cows, two oxen and one bull, and soon they were rich and prosperous and had three sons and a large herd. But one day, so the tale goes, the farmer tapped her three times upon the arm – other tales suggest he her struck three different times – and she left taking her cattle with her back into the lake never to be seen again by anyone but her sons to whom she left a box of her healing potions and the gift of faery healing. Soon 'The Physicians of the Myddfai' were the most respected healers in the land, treating Rhys Gryg, Lord of Dynevor and son of the last native Prince of Wales. When they died they left a large compendium of their healing practice, which can still be accessed today, and a large monastic school of herbal medicine.

Practice: Faery offerings

Those that would be a faery friend should remember the old ways and take up the practice of making offerings. These aren't to assuage negative beings or convince them to treat you well – rather they are gestures of good will and respect, given from the heart. A good faery friend will gain much more from the exchange than they ever need give in offering. All offerings should be biodegradable and leave no trace upon the land and be given as a kindness without expectations of reward. Traditional offerings of butter, milk and cream are good and will most likely be eaten by local wildlife if placed out on the land or in a container that will be collected the next day. Otherwise offerings of song and poetry are also worthy.

To make your offering first decide what offering would be best with generosity and good will in your heart, then find a place that is suitable. This can be in your garden, or on an indoor

altar. Alternatively, this can be somewhere out in nature that feels particularly energetically active or beautiful to you. There are many natural features that are favourite faery places, such as natural springs and wells, oak and elder trees, natural caves as well as ancient sacred sites such as long or round barrows, but suitable places may be found anywhere on earth. Seek out the in-between places – the edge of the hearth, where a spring emerges from the earth or where the shadows meet the light of the sun, and seek out the quiet in-between times to make your gift – the dusk or the dawn, before the rain or as the clouds pass, and as the seasonal wheel turns on the traditional cross quarter days Calan Mai/Beltane and Calan Gaeaf/Samhain, as well as the old feasts of Calan Awst/Lughnasadh and Gŵyl Fair y Canhwyllau/Imbolc. How you give your offerings, what and where will depend on your personal preference and hopefully on your own intuition and experiences of spirit contact, but always take care to leave no litter and to clear any away from a site that you find. Let the shining ones guide you, and may your friendship grow strong.

Practice: Gwyn and the Faery court meditation

Celtic and Brythonic seers, bards and *Awenyddion* – those who seek the wisdom of the Awen – the divine inspiration that reveals the knowledge of all things – have always used their inner vision to encounter the realm of the gods. If we engage our imaginations on a deeper level, and shift our consciousness, they can serve as excellent translation devices between us and spirit, leading us along energetic pathways until we can gain our own way and connect directly. Start this meditation journey to seek Gwyn in your inner vision by creating a sacred space, in whichever way you choose; perhaps by casting a circle, or just lighting a candle, and taking three deep breaths to calm and centre yourself. In your own way call any guides or allies to you that you may choose to work with, even if you do not know them by name – ask for assistance from spirit and it shall come to you. And aloud or in your own mind, state your intention to encounter Gwyn ap Nudd the chief of Annwfn, lord of faery. Try this meditation in the wild lonely places of forest or hillside if you can, or beside a river, but wherever you do it, even at home, be sure the place will be peaceful so that your inner vision is not disturbed.

Feel your feet steady on the ground beneath you, and the breath slow and steady in your lungs. In your inner eye see your feet standing on soft earth, a beaten path across a grassy meadow. Ahead you see a vast green hill stretching up into the sky. Its sides are clothed with dense forest and the air above it shimmers with many colours as if bursts of magical fire are emanating from its summit.

You follow the path across the meadow and see it leads you into a gap in the trees. As soon as you step under the leafy canopy you sense a shift in atmosphere. This is a sacred place, it's as if the trees hide something from sight, and you hear the sound of hooves on soft earth but see nothing. The path pale against the shadows of the trees upon the ground, guides you in a wide arc around the hill, and disappears out of sight in a large spiral. Concentrate on your footsteps, one step after another, and feel the cool air on your cheek and the silent presence of the trees all around.

Eventually your path grows steeper and rockier, and up ahead you see the path terminates not on the summit of the hill, but at a small cavern entrance in its side. A hawthorn tree curls around it and the air is filled with its heady perfume. At the foot of this tree you see a figure sits, calm and still. You cannot see their face, but your skin tingles at the feeling of power all around you in this quiet place.

Walk up to the figure by the entrance, and bow. Greet them politely. They stand and ask you your reason for being here. Answer them honestly, with the first words that arise from your heart. If the guardian is satisfied you may enter the cavern. Remember this is sacred ground, and with every step you draw closer to the heart of the earth. The guardian comes with you to assist with etiquette and can be called upon for advice and guidance to this realm should you need it.

Inside you see that you stand at the beginning of a tunnel. The walls are lined with crystal veins and shimmer in the light of torches. Down the tunnel you go, holding your intention clear in your heart to encounter the faery court.

All at once the tunnel ends and you find yourself in a vast cavern lined with crystal and the deep roots of trees. A pool of water is fed from two small springs emerging from the rock. All around you is the faery host.

They take a myriad of forms, and some of them shift and change and shimmer as you look at them. They may take the forms of animals, trees, shadow and sparkling light, shifting in and out of humanoid form in the blink of an eye. Others are more settled and human in their appearance, regarding you with cool stern eyes, or even mockery. Others smile and greet you kindly. There are others there, ancient ancestors and faery travellers recently passed.

The guardian that has accompanied you leads you to the pool. Go to the water, and in your own way make a prayer to the old gods that you may find wisdom and kindness here. The guardian dips their fingers into the cool surface of the pool and anoints your eyes and your heart with its waters. Do not drink the water even if offered, but thank the guardian and the waters for their gift.

Look about the cavern now, with fresh, blessed eyes and heart.

Across the hall is a throne. Here sits a tall figure with long dark hair. Light radiates from him, dazzling and shimmering. He looks down upon you with bright eyes.

This is Gwyn, lord of Annwfn.

The guardian leads you to the throne. Greet the lord of this realm with a bow and your honest words. Take three deep breaths and try to hold your consciousness here for a while that you may receive his wisdom. Give this plenty of time.

After a while you may be led by the guardian to other places in the hill, or to other features but this should not go on for too long. Soon it will be time to return the way you came and you can ask the guardian to take you back or they may do so anyway.

Return the way you came, up through the tunnel and along the spiral path through the trees. As you emerge from the forest, take a moment to be aware of the change of light and feel your breath in your chest. As you walk across the meadow feel your body more and more until you come to the edge of the meadow and return completely to the everyday world.

Open your eyes and breathe deeply, feeling the air in your lungs hold you to the present time and place. Wriggle your fingers and toes, stamp your feet and take your time to feel fully grounded. You may like to record your experiences in a journal or notebook.

Faeries and ancestors

The realm of faery is always closely connected to the realm of the dead, the two seeming almost indistinguishable in the traditional tales and oral lore. Many a weary traveller or gifted musician tricked or seduced into the faery mounds is said to have seen their dead relatives within their halls, and Annwfn is equally a realm of the ancestors as well as the ever living. This chimes well with the tradition of faery beings living within the hollow hills or barrow mounds of the Neolithic chambered cairns and ritual megalithic sites functioning both as energetic doorways and punctuation points on the landscape around which stories may congregate in the memory of the local inhabitants. Gwyn ap Nudd's dual role as both guardian of Annwfn and leader of the wild hunt as well as King of Faery illustrate this relationship perfectly. According to Crofton Crocker in 1825, one of his titles was 'lord of the cairn' showing that the connection between these sites and the later faery lore was well established and surviving into the nineteenth century.

Gwyn ap Nudd budd buddinawr
Cynt i syrthiai cadoedd rhag Carneddawr
Dy fraiche no brwyn briw i lawr!

Gwyn ap Nudd! Victorious warrior!
How fell the hosts before the dweller of the cairn!
Thy arm like rushes hew'd them down!"[6]

Chapter 3

GWYN AND THE GLASS CASTLE

The legend of Gwyn ap Nudd and St Collen

A sixteenth-century Welsh ecclesiastical manuscript – *Buchedd Collen*, The life of St Collen (Pronounced Cothlenn) discussed the life and works of an early seventh-century Abbot based at the great Abbey at Glastonbury, Somerset. Collen was a Welshman, who after serving as a soldier dedicated himself to service in the abbey and swiftly rose to power. After a time, he decided to become a hermit and lived in a small cell on the side of Glastonbury Tor. It was during his time here that he became aware of Gwyn ap Nudd being worshipped, or at least honoured, by the local people, and eventually encountered Gwyn for himself.

Here is a translation of the text by Lady Charlotte Guest:[7]

And as he was one day in his cell, he heard two men conversing about Gwyn ab Nudd, and saying that he was king of Annwn and of the Fairies. And Collen put his head out of his cell, and said to them, 'Hold your tongues quickly, those are but Devils.' – 'Hold thou thy tongue,' said they, 'thou shalt receive a reproof from him.' And Collen shut his cell as before.

And soon after, he heard a knocking at the door of his cell, and someone inquired if he were within. Then said Collen, 'I am; who is it that asks?' 'It is I, a messenger from Gwyn ab Nudd, the king of Annwn, to command thee to come and speak with him on the top of the hill at noon.'

But Collen did not go. And the next day behold the same messenger came, ordering Collen to go and speak with the king on the top of the hill at noon.

But Collen did not go. And the third day behold the same messenger came, ordering Collen to go and speak with the king

32

on the top of the hill at noon. 'And if thou dost not go, Collen, thou wilt be the worst for it.'

Then Collen, being afraid, arose, and prepared some holy water, and put it in a flask at his side, and went to the top of the hill. And when he came there, he saw the fairest castle he had ever beheld, and around it the best-appointed troops, and numbers of minstrels, and every kind of music of voice and string, and steeds with youths upon them the comeliest in the world, and maidens of elegant aspect, sprightly, light of foot, of graceful apparel, and in the bloom of youth and every magnificence becoming the court of a puissant sovereign. And he beheld a courteous man on the top of the castle, who bade him enter, saying that the king was waiting for him to come to meat. And Collen went into the castle, and when he came there, the king was sitting in a golden chair. And he welcomed Collen honourably and desired him to eat, assuring him that, besides what he saw, he should have the most luxurious of every dainty and delicacy that the mind could desire, and should be supplied with every drink and liquor that his heart could wish; and that there should be in readiness for him every luxury of courtesy and service, of banquet and of honourable entertainment, of rank and of presents: and every respect and welcome due to a man of his wisdom.

'I will not eat the leaves of the trees,' said Collen.

'Didst thou ever see men of better equipment than those in red and blue?' asked the king.

'Their equipment is good enough,' said Collen, 'for such equipment as it is.'

'What kind of equipment is that?' said the king.

Then said Collen, 'The red on the one part signifies burning, and the blue on the other signifies coldness.' And with that Collen drew out his flask, and threw the holy water on their heads, whereupon they vanished from his sight, so that there was neither castle, nor troops, nor men, nor maidens, nor

33

music, nor song, nor steeds, nor youths, nor banquet, nor the appearance of anything whatever, but the green hillocks.

The tale is usually told as if the Saint successfully banished the faeries from the Tor, but a steady study of the text reveals no such success – rather it could easily be seen that as Collen finds himself once more upon 'the green hillocks' it is he who has been banished from the faery court. Perhaps his rudeness to the rather gracious King was duly noted. Of course, the offer of faery food is a notoriously perilous sign of hospitality and it may be that Gwyn and his retinue were inviting Collen into a greater connection with faery than he was bargaining for, their reputation for mischief being well known.

An interesting detail in the tale of Gwyn and Collen is the description of those within the mounds as wearing red and blue. If we dismiss Collen's interpretation that they describe 'burning and coldness' e.g., the fires of hell and the cold of death, or of being outside God's kingdom, we may be reminded that faeries are often associated with the colour red, or seen wearing red, a colour always associated with magic and otherness. In addition to this though we hear within the glass castle they wear the colour blue and Glastonbury itself has close associations with the colour – 'glas' in Welsh means blue/grey and there is evidence to suggest that the inhabitants of the local lake village in the Iron Age wove good quality blue coloured cloth. Some scholars also suggest the name Glastonbury comes from the name of *Cyndrwyn Glas*, Cyndrwyn the blue who was king of the area in the fifth Century, so it may be that those in red and blue are displaying their faery and ancestral connections respectively.

While we know that Collen was an Abbot of Glastonbury around the seventh century, whether his cell was upon the Tor or back in Wales (not far from Glastonbury just across the Severn estuary) is not stated explicitly in the text and still disputed. Several Welsh locations also claim this tale as their own, especially Llangollen which is named after him. However, the connections between Glastonbury Tor and Gwyn remain strong in its earliest name, *Ynys Witrin*, 'the Glass Fortress', being another name for the legendary Caer Wydyr, the Glass Castle, otherwise known as Caer Sidi, the spiral or faery castle and entrance to the Otherworld, as seen in Taliesin's poem *Preiddeu Annwfn*, 'The spoils of Annwn'.

Glastonbury and Caer Wydyr

Glastonbury, a small town in the Somerset marshes just a few miles away from Wales and the Severn estuary is an area rich in myth and magic more than any other in the British landscape, with legends and lore growing all around it like a thicket from the distant past up to the present day. The town stands at the foot of the beautiful Glastonbury Tor, a hill which rises out of the flat landscape around it to the height of 518 feet. Formed of blue lias stone and clay, the conical hill works as a natural aquifer supplying white calcite-rich water and red iron-rich water to the two sacred springs at its base.

Glastonbury has been associated with the otherworldly Isle of Avalon for centuries, surrounded as it is by mists and lakes – once before the land was drained the Tor would have been surrounded by water (a phenomenon still seen after winter rains) and evidence of an Iron Age lake village has provided details of a rich community who for whatever reason seldom set foot on the sacred hill which was known to them as *'Ynys Witrin'*, 'the fortress or of Glass' – synonymous with Caer Wydr, the mound or castle of glass, another name for the Otherworld in the Brythonic tradition, which like the Tor is always reached by crossing water or going through mist.

We first hear of Glastonbury as Ynis Witrin in William of Malmsbury's 'Gesta Regum Anglorum' ('Deeds of the English Kings' c. 1125) and in *The Life of St Gildas*[8] which was also written in the twelfth century based on an earlier ninth-century manuscript. In Gildas we hear of Ynys Witrin as a fortress surrounded by marshes and lakes and the home of a king Melwas who had abducted Queen Guinevere, Arthur's wife who was besieging the castle seeking her return, in a tale obviously parallel to that of Gwyn, Creiddylad and Gwythyr. Interestingly, another thread of Glastonbury lore suggests that the name Ynys Witrin came from a St Gwytherin (victorious) who founded a community on the hill, and the name gradually changed from Ynys Gwytherin to Ynis Witrin. One can hardly mistake the connection there with Gwyn's eternal rival, Gwythyr ap Greidawl.

In Brythonic myth, we hear of the glass castle as one of the many names of the Otherworld, each title conveying one of its properties or functions, and perhaps one of the methods we may use to access it realms. Equally its connection with Avalon is equally old – Avalon was said to be ruled by nine sisters or priestesses, just as the cauldron of Annwfn is ignited or kindled by the breath of nine maidens, showing them to be one and the same. In the heart of this sacred fortress lies the cauldron or sacred vessel of the goddess and it is this which Gwyn guards. While numerous places on the land may be or claim a connection to these Otherworldly destinations – Avalon, for example, is claimed by Glastonbury and the Isle of Lundy among others – it is better to think of these terrestrial locations as especially good places to access Annwfn, the otherworld, rather than expect them to be the destination in and of themselves.

Caer Wydyr and the Brythonic star lore

The Welsh triads tell us that Gwyn ap Nudd was one of the three great astronomers of Britain, the others being Gwydion and Idris – Gwydion the famous magician of Welsh myth and Idris Gawr, Idris the giant son of Gwyddno Garanhir whose seat is the mountain Cader Idris in Snowdonia, the summit of which Idris used for his study of the stars and which is also said to host Gwyn and his wild hunt. Similarly, Gwyn's seat at Glastonbury Tor, and other related areas in the Welsh Black Mountains function well as vantage points for the heavens as well as the land around. Glastonbury Tor's ancient name, Ynys Witrin, connects it closely to Caer Wydr as mentioned in 'the spoils of Annwn' and similarly alludes the study of the heavens, as like those other glass towers of Brythonic myth, Caer Arianrhod, and Merlin/Myrddin's glass tower. These high places function as a still point, the axis mundi from which the ever-turning vastness of space may be considered, as well as the turn of the seasons and relating it also to one of its other names in

Annwfn – Caer Sidi, meaning the faery, or spiral castle. Another possibly later myth related to Glastonbury also relates it to star lore, situating the Tor as the sign of Aquarius in a vast star temple, mapping out the zodiac on the earth itself in a mixture of ancient field boundaries and natural features.

Our Welsh and Brythonic stellar lore is now largely lost but there is no doubt that once this was an area of great significance to the druids and their earlier counterparts. This small selection of stars by their Welsh names demonstrates how important the Brythonic myths were to their star lore and can be used as a basis for further exploration.

Caer Gwydion – the Milky Way
Caer Arianrhod – Corona Borealis
Telyn Arthur – Lyra
Llys Dôn – Cassiopeia

We can see by this list that numerous stellar features were attributed to the gods, and it is likely that at least one or more were once the province of Gwyn a Nudd. The most likely is the constellation of Orion the hunter, arising as he does at Nos Calan Gaeaf/Samhain, to ride high over the skies over the winter months, accompanied by his faithful hound, Dormach/Sirius, the dog star. At Glastonbury in the winter he can be seen striding over the Tor from early evening until the early hours only to recede beneath the horizon as dawn draws near.

Practice: Studying the stars and the solar wheel

There is no doubt that astronomy was of great importance to our ancient ancestors across the British Isles and the whole of Celtic Northern Europe. Many Neolithic structures, barrow mounds and stone circles have alignments to numerous stellar features or mark the solstices and equinoxes, the four cardinal points of the seasonal solar year. Becoming aware of the sun, moon and stars

and their great cycles leads us into ever greater awareness of the
vast rhythms of life on the land and our place within it, and in turn
the universe itself. There are many books that can guide you with
this lore, and now there are hundreds of computer programmes
and apps that can help you locate and identify the stars above you,

and what stellar features would have or still do align with any position on earth at any time in the future or distant past – useful if you wish to explore archaeoastronomy or visit sacred sites and see what stellar alignments they may have had at the time of their construction.

In Celtic faery lore, there are many tales of people seeing stars within the earth itself, and in an example of the old adage 'as above so below' careful exploration of Annwfn and the inner realms of the land via seership and inner vision do have the potential to allow the seeker to encounter ever greater beings and an increasing sense of vast space – as if the whole universe may be accessed by going 'within' – indeed modern faery encounters can even have a great deal in common with alien and UFO sightings.

Let the presence of the stars and their slow reel across the heavens fill your consciousness. On a calm clear night, climb to a high place, and lie back upon the earth, letting your body sink into the soil as your spirit soars to the greatest heights. Let your mind and eyes wander, counting the stars and letting your senses expand into the great endless expanse before you. Allow yourself to drift on their silver currents, letting the hours pass without care or conscious study. See if you can feel their great presences and in contrast the blue-green gem upon which you dwell. Allow their poetry, their endless song, to tangle in your hair and permeate your whole being for a while, and ignite the *Awen*, the inspirational and oracular fires within you.

In the winter months seek out, especially, Orion the hunter, and greet this giant each night as he strides across the sky. Allow his presence to be a part of your awareness, and mark his passing through the night as a prayer to guide your way through the winter, whether the cold season be within the land or within your own soul. Know his great strength as he walks through the darkness, and know him as your ally and guide, not in the mind, but in the heart, where your courage may be found.

Chapter 4

GWYN AND THE MABINOGION

The earliest written collection of prose tales in Britain, the Mabinogion, or *Tales for Boys*, is dated to the twelfth to thirteenth centuries. Compiled from earlier manuscripts and traditional oral lore, the Mabinogion – or more accurately, the *Mabinogi* are a collection of eleven tales recorded mainly in the White Book of Rhydderch (c. 1350) and The Red Book of Hergest (c. 1400) where we encounter the realm of Annwfn in wonderful detail.

In what is usually called 'the first branch' we encounter '*The tale of Pwyll Prince of Dyfed*' and meet the King of Annwfn, named here as Arawn, which is likely to be another name for Gwyn, perhaps drawing on his other earthier attributes – the name Arawn may come from the Celtic for 'Tiller' or 'God of the ploughed field'. Gwyn is explicitly mentioned more fully in *The Tale of Culhwch and Olwen* which is also part of the collection, and which we will cover in some detail.

The tale of Pwyll Prince of Dyfed

Pwyll is hunting when he comes across the Cŵn Annwfn, the faery hounds, and takes their kill – a white stag – for himself. The leader of the Cŵn Annwfn, Arawn then appears and is mightily offended. As an act of recompense Pwyll agrees to swap places with Arawn for one year and defeat his enemy Hagfan for him. During this time, he is also to share a bed with Arawn's wife, without touching her once. Arawn's wife is not named in the tale, but functions as both a goddess and a symbol of sovereignty and the soul of the land over which Arawn, as a double for Gwyn ap Nudd, is guardian. As a result of this Pwyll learns responsibility and self-restraint, and perhaps even to control a Celtic form of kundalini, which is hinted at in numerous other tales, such as in the Irish examples of training the Fianna and Cúchulainn's battle frenzy. Pwyll learns to control his baser urges be they sexual or otherwise and becomes a worthy and honourable king due to the experience. He is granted a great alliance with Arawn and on his return, notes that Arawn has ruled his earthly kingdom well in his absence. The tale as a whole can be seen as a manual for spiritual training – by communing with but still holding as sacred, the goddess of the land herself, one learns wisdom and a deeper soulful communion with the earth in its spirit form. One discovers the vivifying currents which can sustain rightful sovereignty within oneself and on behalf of others.

The Tale of Culhwch and Olwen

Later in the Mabinogion is the Tale of Culhwch and Olwen. Culhwch (culoowk) is the cousin of King Arthur, and enlists his help in order to win the hand of the maiden Olwen. Olwen 'white footprint' is the daughter of Yspadadden Penncawr, 'King of giants' and is said to be so beautiful that white flowers spring up under her feet. Yspadadden sets Culhwch over forty impossible tasks to prove his worthiness to marry Olwen, and Arthur grants Culhwch several of his men in order to complete the challenges. One of these tasks is to hunt a huge magical boar named *Trwch Trwyth* who is himself the son of a prince under enchantment and who can only be slain with the help of Gwyn ap Nudd. *Twrch Trwyth*, or 'the boar named Trwyth', has poisonous bristles and carries a pair of scissors, a razor and a comb between his ears. Trwyth may be cognate with the Irish *Triath*, making his name 'king of boars' (Old Irish *Triath ri torcraide*) which could place him as the same magical Boar, the Torc Triath mentioned in *Lebor Gabála Érenn, the book of the Taking of Ireland,* the great body of Irish creation myth.

Boars in Celtic myth as in nature are fierce creatures, and their appearance in tales usually signifies leadership and responsibility, even royalty, but there is always something Otherworldly or underworldly going on as well. Boar imagery in Iron Age Celtic art is connected to ideas of war and images of boars or boar tusks were popular on warrior's helmets. Boars in nature are usually very shy creatures, and the tutelary goddess of the Ardennes forest in France, Arduinna who is depicted riding a boar most likely represents the power and sovereignty of her land for its wild as well as its human inhabitants in peaceful balance, without any negative connotations. Later a recurring motif was for boars to represent the chthonic underworld forces of chaos and darkness which were sacrificed or defeated by the new or light gods or heroes. Yspadadden in the tale has one of his servants lift up his eye with a fork, and this may be reminiscent of the solar imagery which can be seen in the Irish tale of Balor of the baleful eye, which requires a chain to open it. Balor, like Yspadadden wants to deny his daughter a husband as it would bring on his demise, and is defeated in the end by the new god Lugh, his grandson, in a new sun god beats old sun god motif which is seen repeatedly across Northern Europe. It may be that Culhwch defeating the boar, and thus in effect defeating Yspadadden's challenge, repeats this pattern in the Welsh tale. Culhwch also, like Lugh, pierces the giant's eye with a spear, although in the Welsh tale, unlike the Irish this isn't fatal. The character of Yspadadden as well as the great boar can also be read as the quest to defeat the old pagan gods and war leaders in favour of a more-courtly Christianised ideal represented by Arthur and his retinue, the pivotal character of Culhwch facilitating the change but having equal investment in both worlds.

Boars, like pigs in Celtic myth also have healing and visionary qualities and are often associated with the figure of the divine madman or prophet, who seeks a living as a swineherd in the forest outside of the human world. The name Culhwch is also connected to pigs and boars, as it is thought to mean 'pig run', or even pigsty – the name given to him as it was the place of his birth, suggesting he lives upon the cusp of this world and the next.

Gwyn ap Nudd enters this tale as an essential companion when hunting for the boar alongside his eternal rival Gwythyr ap Greidawl. The boar, as already mentioned, is actually a prince under enchantment, a son of Prince Tarred Wledig, but there is no freeing him from the curse. He rages across the land and the task of his hunters is to seize the razor, scissors and comb from his head to appease Yspadadden before chasing him into the sea. Later in the tale another, the chief of boars, Ysgithyrwyn is also hunted for his tusk, his primal power. To see Gwyn in this hunt, mentioned as essential to the task hints at his role as psychopomp, representing and overseeing the death process, freeing the prince from his enchantment by returning him to the sea, and Annwfn, where he can restore and prepare for his next life.

Sovereignty and the eternal battle

In the Mabinogion, the tale of Culhwch and Olwen takes many meandering turns in order to tell the tales of various other characters as the story progresses, and one such is the eternal love triangle of Gwyn, Gwythyr and the maiden Creiddylad.

Creiddylad we are told in the tale is the daughter of Lludd LLaw Erient – Lludd being another version of Nudd/Nuada/Nodens, yet here the etymology gets tangled, and Lludd is also often taken to be another name for LLyr – the sea god, cognate with the Irish Lir. Gwythyr ap Greidawl (Victor son of scorcher) is due to marry Creiddylad, who is described as 'the most majestic maiden there ever was'[9] yet Gwyn abducts her before the marriage is consummated. Gwythyr raises an army against Gwyn, but is defeated, and several of his noblemen are captured. Two of his prisoners are Nwython and his son Cyledr and in a curious development Gwyn in his fury kills Nwython and forces his son Cyledr to eat his heart. Cyledr is driven mad by this and gains the epithet *Wyllt* (wild) upon his name – suggesting he undertakes a magical/spiritual transformation into a visionary and prophet.

Gwythyr ap Greidawl, victor, son of scorcher, may be understood as having solar and sky attributes as well as representing summer, scorcher being likely to refer to the sun. As such we can imagine him as active in the mortal or upper world realms, a character concerned with fertility, heroism, youth and the gaining of prestige in the mortal world – through being active in life. In contrast, Gwyn as lord of Annwfn places him firmly in the inner or underworld, where self-awareness, transformation and transmutation takes place, where the soul is tempered and matured. All this inner growth takes place beneath the surface of things, and this together with his connection to Nos Calan Gaeaf/ Samhain (Oct 31st) and the wild hunt and his role as psychopomp place him firmly in the seasonal wheel in the place of winter. King Arthur places himself as the ultimate arbiter of their duel and condemns them to fight every 1st of May (Calan Mai/Beltane) for Creiddylad's hand until the end of time, in a pattern echoing the seasonal wheel of the land ever turning from summer to winter and back again.

Creiddylad, despite being called 'majestic' is less easy to interpret. Creiddylad's name seems to defy translation, but we see from her lineage that she is born from either the god of the sea, or the inner depths of dream/mist/cloud/firmament of Nudd/ Nuada. Both these gods are concerned with an in-between state, some place outside of the quantifiable matter and physicality of the mortal world. Yet she herself is described as 'majestic' – having majesty. This links her irrefutably with that perennial concept in Celtic lore – that of sovereignty, the royal soul of the land which appears in many tales and is usually embodied by a female figure. During the eternal battle for her hand, King Arthur states that she returns to her father's kingdom until such time as the matter is settled.

The fact that Gwyn's father is also Nudd/Lludd/Nuada/Nodens is not mentioned in the tale. He is not named as her brother and it may be that the connection between Lludd and Nudd was overlooked or considered to be of no consequence – certainly this isn't a matter of incest or brotherly jealousy, rather an enticing clue into a long-lost initiation and mystery teaching.

That Gwythyr and Gwyn battle over her, in what can be understood as an eternal struggle between winter and summer and that she seems to arise from an Otherworldly and intangible spirit state to touch the mortal world only briefly seems to add weight to her as an embodiment of sovereignty and soul, one that infuses the land with life but is none the less held beyond it in a seemingly timeless space within the land. That Gwyn is never defeated by Gwythyr places him in a similar position, dwelling in the centre and heart of the land and arising out of it to encounter the challenge from Gwythyr, an external (solar) force from a place of still centrality rather than a linear or ever-turning exchange of places.

In the tales of Gwyn ap Nudd, Creiddylad is an elusive figure. In the Mabinogion all we have to describe her is that she is 'majestic' and that she is 'betrothed' to Gwythyr and kidnapped by Gwyn before returning to her father, Lludd. In the dialogue of Gwyn ap Nudd and Gwyddno Garanhir we have the additional detail that Gwyn is her 'lover' – note he says *he* is the lover of Creiddylad, not that she is *his* – implying his love and respect rather than any sense of ownership. At no point does he call himself the captor of Creiddylad. We also know in oral tradition from the fourteenth century that she was called his queen and was invoked in seeking permission to enter his kingdom – the wild wood.

...to the king of Spirits, and to his queen – Gwyn ap Nudd, you who are yonder in the forest, for love of your mate, permit us to enter your dwelling.[10]

Again, here Gwyn's love for her, and her implied generous nature give us hints as to her personality or identity, and her relationship with him.

If looking at the Gwyn-Gwythyr-Creiddylad triangle from a feminist perspective she may seem powerless and unrepresented – certainly, we never hear her voice or will. That said we must remember that this tale was written down in the mid-thirteenth century, and although it is likely based on far older oral sources, the language and structure of the tale is based in that context. As such the courtly maiden is silent while male protagonists battle for her hand and we can only infer her preferences in the matter. Certainly, if we consider it on the level of human relations we know that while she may be betrothed to Gwythyr this indicates nothing of her feelings or lack of them for him, and the same can be said for Gwyn. It may be that as he is elsewhere termed her lover there may have been earlier lost versions of the tale where their relationship was more explicit, either sharing mutual affection or as kidnapper and victim. Equally Gwythyr may have been her favourite, or neither. It may even be somewhere in between – as a pagan mystery tale it may reflect the emotional and sexual complexities of a wild and soulful female protagonist – or the eternally shifting affections of nature herself – she may love them both each in their season. What we do know is that the fragments remaining and later folk tradition make Gwythyr very much the third wheel in this triangular relationship, and that for the most part we can view Creiddylad, in the context of the tales at least, as being either Gwyn's queen – he after all wins the battle against Gwythyr despite its annual rematch, or that she dwells mainly in the third place – the realm of her father Lludd.

There is, however, another less analytical way to explore the nature of Creiddylad if we view her with the eyes of the soul and inner knowing. If we consider her father to be the Lludd/Nudd/ Nuada/Nodens who has his roots in the tradition of divinatory dreaming, and the in-between ethereal realm of clouds and mist and lunar corresponding silver hands, we see she must have her origins in some place infused with spirit. Just as Gwyn's name means white or blessed/holy, it may be that Creiddylad's name whose meaning is now forgotten may once have had related connotations – certainly they seem to share the same source.

The idea that Gwyn and Creiddylad may be brother and sister

never arises in the tales or oral lore and this is significant, as other familial relationships are clearly related and even rape and incest is touched upon in other tales in the Mabinogion, so we know those writing down the stories weren't averse to including these details. There are also precedents in other cultures where brother and sister gods appear to be couples – the Egyptian Isis and Osiris is perhaps the most famous but others can be found around the world. In the Brythonic lore, we have it that Gwyn is the son of Nudd and Creiddylad is the daughter of Lludd and while these are both forms of the same originating deity this fact appears to be overlooked by those writing the tales. It may also be that their familial relationship isn't the point – that to share this father is not the same as it would be in a mortal human relationship – rather, that, as the name Nudd and Lludd suggests, they both emerged from the mists, through the veil between the Otherworld and this.

If we see Creiddylad in this context, as an Otherworldly woman who none the less represents or even embodies the figure of sovereignty then we must understand her not as a medieval female character or a figure of Celtic myth in merely narrative terms. We can view her as a being who moves to and fro between the worlds, drawing Otherworldly energy with her and imbuing this quality into the land she represents – that she embodies not the physical matter of the land but its spirit representative, its soul. Thus, her return through the misty veil returns her to the spirit world, the realm of Annwfn guarded by her 'lover' Gwyn, but her role to bless and bring fertility to the land continues year on year as she emerges at Calan Mai/Beltane, and Gwyn and Gwythyr battle for her hand, to recede back to 'the deep place' of Annwfn within the heart of the land every time Gwyn eventually wins, presumably at Nos Calan Gaeaf/Samhain when we see him ascendant once again.

The two-faced god

There is another way to understand the relationships between Gwyn, Gwythyr and Creiddylad, when we take into consideration the prolific two- or sometimes three-faced 'Janus figures' found across the Iron Age Celtic world. Stone sculptures such as those found on Boa Island, Ireland are fascinating sculptures, featuring two distinct figures facing in opposite directions with their bodies merging into one. Others such as the one found in Roquepertuse, France (600-124 BCE) are just the heads, with a stone vessel between them perhaps for receiving offerings and libations. While these sculptures are usually called 'Janus' figures, after the Roman god of Doorways, beginnings and endings – hence looking in both directions, they are often now thought to be representations of a pre-Roman Celtic god or gods – the two faces representing the duality of their nature. It may be that Gwyn and Gwythyr in their eternal struggle are a natural pair or two sides of the older deity, Vindonnus-Belenus, concerned with life and death, winter and summer, youth and age etc., one side in Annwfn or the underworld, the other in the upper world/solar/sky, each aspect serving the goddess in turn.

Practice: Meeting Gwythyr

In this meditation journey, we will use our inner vision to seek the council of Gwythyr ap Greidawl 'Victor son of Scorcher' to seek wisdom and encounter the virile solar currents that fertilize the earth.

This exercise is best performed with the sun on your face, or with the heat of a fire or the flicker of candlelight before you which you may sense through your closed eyelids.

First sitting upright, close your eyes and take three deep breaths. Call to your guides and spiritual allies, whether you know them by name or not, trust that they attend you, then state your intention out loud to seek an encounter with Gwythyr.

See yourself standing in a great stone archway, with a clear, dry, dusty path ahead of you leading up a broad hillside in the heat of summer. The grass is dry although still green, insects buzz low through the upright stems of cowslip and hemlock flowers and settle lazily on the deep green leaves of elder and hazel that spring up here and there along your route. Gradually as you walk you see you are leaving a lowland meadow and climb higher into the craggy hillside, and the trees become larger as if you enter into gradually wilder terrain. You notice there are many large oak trees here and there around you and the leathery green of holm oak and holly leaves lends brief moments of shade along the path. You go further and the trees open up to high moorland and vast swathes of broom and golden gorse blossom surround you together with rough purple heather. The sky above is bright blue and cloudless and the deep heat of summer beats down upon you.

Ahead you see that the line of the hillside above you flickers with golden light, and a heat haze shimmers in the air above the horizon line. As you grow nearer you hear the crackle and snapping sounds of fire on the hillside. The gorse and heather are aflame.

You carry on the path, aware that there is danger here, that while there is no wind the path of the fire is predictable, but it could change at any moment. You are not afraid, but there is a sense of drama and excitement in the air, a fierceness in the flame that draws you forward and yet sets your heart racing. You pause and call your guides and allies to you once more, and only continue should you feel it is appropriate to proceed.

As you rise to the next level of the hills you see the fire has spread across a whole field of gorse and heather and the golden flames and golden blooms seem to turn and transform one into the other and back again in fluid fiery motion. Though there are areas of rich black burnt earth here and there where the fire has receded, it seems that from where you stand the whole hill is afire. The air tingles and shimmers with heat and your eyes find it hard to focus for a moment, and then across the hill you see the figure of a man striding through the flame. His hair is golden red and his strong arms swinging free of a golden-brown tunic are strongly muscled and visibly shimmer with sweat. As he walks towards you through the flames you realise this miraculous figure is far taller than any man and though he walks through the fiercest flames he is unburnt. As he gets nearer you see that as he raises his hands through the gorse the plants shoot upward into new green life, burst into golden blossom and then crackle and explode into flames all at his touch. Far behind him, the dark earth of the burnt hillside grows steadily, and then turns green with new life like a great verdant wave.

The man pauses a few feet from you, and the fire seems to calm. Instead new growth shoots from the gorse and blossoms golden all around him. You look up into his face and you see his cheeks are flushed and his amber eyes glow with life.

This is Gwythyr, lord of summer fire. He knows the secrets of heat and light and regeneration but also the powers of fire and fury.

Spend some time here in his company, feel the heat that radiates from him. He may have advice for you about how to seize your own victories, or how to handle your own passion and energy better. It may be that there are parts of you or your life that you would offer to his flames for transformation, and you can seek his wisdom and assistance on this also. Remember though to always be respectful in case his warmth should turn into destroying fire.

When you are ready thank Gwythyr for his wisdom, and bow your head briefly in respect. Return the way you came down through the hills and back through the stone archway, returning to your body gently and easily.

Feel the breath in your chest, and breathe in and out a few times, and wiggle your fingers and toes to feel yourself back firmly in your body. You may like to record your experiences in a journal.

Afterwards, you may like to have a special pillar candle that you can light repeatedly in honour of Gwythyr whenever you seek his wisdom or support, and when you are low in physical energy and health to attract more of his robust energy and light into your life. You may also call upon him when you seek victory in a dispute, as long as that which you seek is just, not against your own inner nature, or the deep wisdom of nature herself.

Encountering sovereignty

The figure of sovereignty appears throughout Celtic and Arthurian lore. Representing the soul and heart of the land, as well as being its incarnate goddess she is a figure often mistreated and misunderstood, battled over by dual forces of summer and winter, good and evil, youth and age, or denigrated, denied and abused by a single male protagonist until he finally acknowledges her worth or succumbs to her vengeance. Her appearance varies, and how she is 'seen' by the protagonists of the tales tells us a lot about their attitude to her and their relationship to the land, as well as their own inner lives. She's often a woman, often beautiful, but this is only her friendly face, in many ways her most passive stance as the figure over which others fight. Sometimes she's ancient and ugly, often when others need lessons in humility or need to restore honour. But sometimes she's an animal, such as a horse or a swan, and there is something especially ancient here as if the call to discover her means more than encountering the spirit or soul version of the mortal world – to encounter her we must encounter the wilder self, the animal self and we are reminded she oversees the *whole* of the land not only human affairs. She appears in both the Brythonic, Irish and Scots literature and oral tales, and can be traced right through into Proto-Indo-European culture, found as far afield as India and Sumeria in the tales of Vishnu and Lakshmi, Dumuzi and Inanna. In Arthurian sagas she has many guises, most commonly in Guinevere as well as being embodied and symbolised by the grail – here the cup of Christ is transposed upon that more ancient symbol of womb-like sacred vessel the cauldron.

In Celtic culture, the figure of sovereignty was represented by numerous earth and mother goddesses who bestowed health and fertility on the land, and evidence suggests that rites of sacred kingship involved ritually or physically mating with her in order to achieve legitimacy. It is argued by some scholars that in Ireland such kings may even have had a set term or lifespan before being sacrificed to her – the evidence of bog bodies – possibly the victims of ritual killings preserved in the peat bogs below hills used for ritual, could point to this among other interpretations.[11] However, that such a tradition persisted in Ireland at least until relatively recent times is attested to in the work of Giraldus Cambrensis. In his *Topographia Hibernica* (1188) Cambrensis makes no attempt to hide his disgust at the installation of the *Ard Ri* – the High King at

Tara which involved the king's sexual contact with a white mare who embodied the sovereignty of the land as part of the rituals known as the *feis temrach* and *fled bainisi*.

In the tale of Culhwch and Olwen we see sovereignty appear in several guises as this tale of tales weaves in a myriad of other related lore. In many ways Olwen is a version of sovereignty – her love is a hard-won prize – but we really see sovereignty revealed in the figure of Creiddylad, fought over every Calan Mai/Beltane (May 1st) by Gwyn and Gwythyr, the night and day, winter and summer, under and upper world guardians and representatives, in their endless battle for her hand.

In some ways sovereignty is something that is always fought for; it cannot come easily from birthright or any political system. It is a place of harmony and balance where all is literally 'all right with the world', a state of blessedness and heavenly wholeness. However, this state must be continually in flux. If it was to stay forever there would be no growth, no maturing, no sense that it was to be valued and honoured. It is a state of spirit; its place is in the realms of the divine not the mortal world yet the quest to bring it to the mortal world is a divinely ordained one whereby wisdom and a soulful life may be achieved. Sovereignty must come, and in its time return from whence it came just as Creiddylad returns to her father – to be reclaimed during the next cycle, or by the next generation. Sovereignty, soul, connection with the goddess or finding the grail must by its very nature be a prize not an entitlement and those who seek it must know its value – in fact knowing its value is the prize itself – its attainment is a recognition or re-remembering of the soul, a return to the senses where the beauty and sanctity of the land becomes visible once again and our relationship to that divine state is restored.

To find sovereignty in our own lives is a continuous journey and one that will need to be repeated over and over for most people as our connection to it waxes and wanes and waxes once again. At first, especially with the enthusiasm and confidence of youth such an attainment may seem easy, it may even appear as if no quest or battle is required. This is most often, however, a state of naivety rather than sovereignty – a presumption that no work needs doing, that there is nothing waiting in the shadows. With time, however, we see how life saps us of sovereignty, drains it away with daily concerns or denies us enough power over our own destinies to encounter such a vivifying presence, and so the quest must begin. If we are not sovereign in our own lives we can be sure that someone or something else is, and that must be tackled if we are to marry the queen of the land or finally recover our own soul's treasure.

On a wider perspective, regionally and nationally, sovereignty is even more complex – our mortal kings and queens and political structures may claim sovereignty of one sort or another but it's unlikely they could ever be considered to represent the goddess of the earth or her consort, unless it is as a means of creating moving propaganda to stir the hearts of the population; as a tool of control not as a way to vivify and bless the land or to restore health and wholeness for all creation. There is something universally stirring about sovereignty that pulls on every heart but sadly the days of royalty and other leaders serving as go-betweens, enacting the sacred marriage as the bond between the people and the gods, is long gone, if it ever was other than in myth. Instead sovereignty is an elusive figure, something that calls to us with an inner yearning, something that will wake us in the night or stir us to tears at a sunset but is easily over looked in the brash light of day. What we are left with are tales, examples and clues to help us each forge this bond, defeat our counter point and follow this quest ourselves until we finally hold the goddess in our arms, or our own soul is restored once again. We do this by learning to hear our inner voice, the wisdom of our own heart – becoming 'true of heart' as the old tales say and following the energetic and fateful streams of what is inherently healthy and wholesome back to the Source.

Practice: The dark mirror. Seeking wisdom from the unseen

In this meditation journey, we will seek a vision from the dark mirror, the waters of Annwfn, to better know ourselves, and to let go of what no longer serves our growth and healing, that we may be better prepared to meet our sovereignty and wholeness.

This is best performed somewhere quiet where you are comfortable but will remain uninterrupted for at least half an hour.

First sitting upright, close your eyes and take three deep breaths. Call to your guides and spiritual allies, whether you know them by name or not, trust that they attend you, then state your intention out loud to seek an encounter with the waters of Annwfn.

In your inner vision see that it is dusk, and you stand on a narrow path between low trees. You follow the path as the light fades, until it opens onto an expanse of reeds and willow trees, rising taller than your head, so that your view is limited. The air smells damp and is full of the sounds of marshes, of croakings and chirrups and the lonely call of geese gathering out of sight. The path leads you onwards, until it forms a narrow trackway of split timbers supported by timber posts pushed crosswise into the marshy waters. On either side you can see through the reeds and weeds, dark water beneath and around you. You must step slowly and carefully, one foot after another.

Let your inner vision focus on your feet, while all around is darkening, one step after another, slow as a drum beat. Your breathing also slows to match the rhythm so you seem to glide slowly, carried on your breath along the narrow way, as if along a thread.

Suddenly ahead you see the path widens into a platform upon the waters, and you see you are breaking clear of the reeds and the path has lead you through to open water. Night has gathered in now and above you the sky is brilliant with stars. Everything is so still and quiet, you can see them reflected clearly upon the water. The effect is strange, and disorientating but very beautiful, as if you stand upon the edge of space. Above you the constellation of Orion stands tall, with the dog star Sirius at his heel. Below they are perfectly reflected. Take a moment to consider this vision, breathing slow and let its inner magic work upon you.

"What do you sacrifice in this ancient place?" The voice shocks you from your meditation, and you see a figure in the darkness, standing a few feet away. You guess that it is a man by the tone of their voice, but they are completely shrouded, wrapped in black, their face is hidden or darkened by paint and ashes so that only the glimmer of their eyes can be seen. How do you answer? What are you willing to let go of at this time? Something appears in your hand, it may be an object or something else, perhaps something symbolising a thought, a feeling or a memory. The figure takes it from you and looks at it carefully, he may have words of insight or guidance for you, before handing it back.

"Give it with your care to the waters," he commands. You kneel at the edge of the platform and place your object carefully into the lake. To your surprise, you see too that your reflection can be clearly seen, as if you reach up from the darkness to take the gift from yourself. Your hands shift and distort as they are seen through the water, and you let your sacrifice go, sinking into the blackness in front of you. "Now, look well and look deep," commands the figure, and you take a moment to study your own face reflected as if in a dark mirror. Other images may also pass before you. What do you see? Are you the same as in the daylight world? Here you may find another truth.

"This is your gift from the waters," says the man, who you know now to be the guardian of this ancient place. And you know that the wisdom of your vision is a gift indeed, though it may take some time to know its meaning.

You rise slowly, and bow your head in respect of this strange teacher. Give him your thanks and return the way you came. Follow the track through the marshes and the trees, focusing on your breathing, until you see the trees fade and your sense of your body grows stronger once again.

You see you have returned to your body far quicker and easier than your outward journey. Take your time, wriggle your fingers and toes and let your consciousness return gently and fully.

Practice: Meeting Creiddylad

In this meditation journey, we will seek the council of Creiddylad daughter of Lludd, mysterious goddess of spring and sovereignty.

This exercise is best performed somewhere quiet where you are comfortable but will remain uninterrupted for at least half an hour.

First sitting upright, close your eyes and take three deep breaths. Call to your guides and spiritual allies, whether you know them by name or not – trust that they attend you, then state your intention out loud to seek an encounter with Creiddylad.

In your inner vision see yourself standing at a great stone archway, and ahead of you is a simple path of pale stone and soft earth, winding its way along a tunnel of hawthorn trees. You step out onto the path and the light around you is soft and blue – you cannot tell if it is dusk or early dawn but there is a cool freshness in the air and the scent of green leaves and good earth. Ahead of you swoops the pale shape of an owl hunting, though you do not hear her lonely call. As you follow the path, the way ahead is dappled in light and shade – deep impenetrable shadows and the lighter areas seem to shimmer silver, and you sense that indeed dawn is near. Overhead the branches of the trees begin to sigh in a soft breeze and you are startled to hear a heavy shuffling noise to your right – you turn your head but cannot see its source. You let your eyes grow more accustomed to the light and you begin to see through the hawthorn branches into the space beyond. In between the tree trunks and twigs you realise you can see a large field, a huge grassy mound arcing off ahead of you and alongside the path you are on. In the field, just a few feet away a beautiful white horse is standing, head bowed munching on some fresh grass. It raises its perfect silver head to gaze at you with large steady eyes. You take a moment to gaze at the beautiful white mare.

When you feel it is time you continue on your way along the path, which rises steadily before opening out onto the base of a large steep hill, a conical mound that reaches up to the sky, its sides wreathed here and there with morning mist. The pale path spirals around the side of the hill and carries you steadily to its summit.

When you finally stand on the top of the hill, the vast expanse of the land around you is staggering – all around you see emerging, as if from a white cloud, rolling hills and distant mountains, you see lakes and deep forests, open plains and further off the amber glow of streetlights and houses, lining the far horizon with deep golden light, ever flickering, never still, like distant fire.

Suddenly the wind stirs your hair and you hear distant bells chiming, small and delicate yet clear through the cool blue air. You follow the sound and look down at the foot of the hill beneath you. The white mare still stands tall and proud in the green field, but now the air shimmers about her as if a great unseen faery host swirls all around. In the distance, you see a woman dressed in white striding over the land, she seems impossibly tall, crossing whole fields in one step, yet she is delicate and graceful in all her movements. All around her there is a shimmer and a shift in the air, a great warm sigh in the earth although nothing shakes or is broken. There is a change which you feel in your very blood but is impossible to define, or describe. It is as if the land itself rejoices and blooms and grows rich at her passing, where her feet tread the land becomes somehow more real, more alive in your vision.

Her voice comes clear and cool through the blue air.

"Why do you seek me child of earth?" You were not aware that she had climbed the hill, yet she stands before you now. Her eyes are calm and clear, her soft brown hair glints with gold as the sun begins to rise. Your heart thuds in your chest. Let it speak your truth to her now, in this most sacred place.

She may grant you wisdom, or She may not, but either way

take this moment to connect with this most majestic maiden, for She has much to teach if She is willing, and if you are able to hear.

After a while it may be clear or you may feel that your audience with Creiddylad is coming to its close. Thank Her for her wisdom, and bow your head briefly in respect. Return the way you came down the hill and back through the hawthorn tunnel to the stone archway, returning to your body gently and easily.

Feel the breath in your chest, breathe in and out a few times, and wiggle your fingers and toes to feel yourself back firmly in your body. You may like to record your experiences in a journal.

Afterwards, you may like to have a special pillar candle that you can light repeatedly in honour of Creiddylad whenever you seek her wisdom or blessing. You may also like to make her regular offerings of flowers upon an altar in your home or in some other sacred space. Remember that any gift or offerings that you make should be heartfelt and always sure to do no harm to the land or any form of life.

Into the Wyllt – Gwyn and Cyledr

There is a final twist to the tale of Gwyn and Gwythyr in the Mabinogion and one that takes the narrative into far darker and more ancient territory. Gwyn overcomes Gwythyr in battle and seizes several of his men – two of these are Nwython and Cyledr, father and son.

In an unusual act Gwyn kills Nwython – whose name could mean great sky or air, or possibly be related to the modern word Nwyth meaning eccentric or odd, and makes his son Cyledr eat his father's heart, driving him mad. Cyledr whose name is likely to have forest or wilderness connotations, possibly related to Caledonia – the forest of the goddess Dôn – gains the title *Wyllt* or wild from the experience, denoting his changed status to that of a Wildman or visionary living outside of society. Others in the Brythonic tradition and in the Irish and Scots have similar titles, most famously Myrddin/Merlin who gains the title Myrddin

Wyllt during his phase as a Wildman of the woods struggling with insanity and grief inducing visions and prophetic frenzy.

Positioned in a medieval tale, albeit a version of much earlier material, this example of forced cannibalism has disturbing overtones, and can be challenging material in the modern era. However, it is likely to be a tiny scrap of a tale or even a tradition that is far older and taken out of context. There is evidence of Celtic warriors honouring the body parts of their enemies, using them as objects of power, and hearts and entrails may have been used for divinatory purposes, suggesting a belief that the blood and viscera could be used as a gateway to access divine knowledge. Earlier in the Neolithic era there is limited evidence of cannibalism as a ritual act, to consume the power of the ancestors perhaps, and as in later traditions worldwide cannibalism can be understood as an act of honouring a loved one, just as it can be seen as an act of domination by consuming the power of a fallen foe. The names of the father and son, with their implications of either sky and forest, or madness/eccentricity and forest, and given their alignment with the solar/upper world Gwythyr represents suggest something more mythical and symbolic may be taking place than mere vengeance. That they, with Gwyn's other captives, are held prisoner – presumably in Annwfn – suggests that Cyledr is undergoing an initiatory cycle perhaps, a ritual of descent and ultimate rebirth. In this context Cyledr eating his father's heart may be understood as consuming his power or his ancestral legacy, and undergoing a prophetic and inspired transformation as a result.

The Wyllt or Wildman

Cyledr's transformation into Wildman is a recurring motif in the Celtic tradition, where such figures are often carriers of great wisdom and power, and can even represent the spirits of the land and the wild themselves, such as the Scots *Gruagach,* or the later *Woodwose.* Sometimes becoming a man of the wild wood is a transition to bring eventual healing along with wisdom, such

as when Myrddin Wyllt/Merlin Silvestris goes mad and lives in the wood after the battle of Arfderydd, a tale which in turn was drawn from the Scottish figure of Lailoken. For these characters, their time in the woods represents a merging with its peace and distance from the world of men and its events. Their time there may be full of grief and vision, but it is a healing journey overall.

At other times, these beings are spirit or faery in nature, having never been part of the human world rather dwelling alongside it in the remote wilderness. These beings are even more at one with the land itself, dwelling closer to or even in Annwfn at places where it intersects with or overlays the human realm.

That so many wildmen, and sometimes wildwoman figures utter poetry and prophecy in these tales is testimony to the lasting influence of the bardic tradition on the medieval monks who usually recorded them, from either earlier manuscripts or oral lore. As the pagan druid tradition eased over centuries into the Christian era much of the lore was retained in the monasteries and a limited knowledge of the bardic mysteries survived albeit in a disjointed and broken form. Poetry in this sense has its roots not so much in literary endeavour as we understand it today as an expression of divine inspiration where poetry was used to utter prophecy and weave magic. This divine inspiration always has is roots and source in the land. A close relationship with nature and the spirit or soul of the landscape embodied as a goddess or lady sovereignty induces an initiatory sequence where a descent into darkness beneath the earth or a period of madness breaks down the rational mind to allow access to the spirit realm and the inner vision of the soul.

Other than Myrddin, the most famous Bard in the Brythonic tradition was the semi-divine figure of Taliesin, whose name means 'radiant brow'. Taliesin was both the name of a real-world Bard in sixth- century Wales, or at least a series of bards assuming that name, and a mythical magical figure who underwent a magical initiation with the goddess Cerridwen. In his birth and initiation tale Cerridwen is the keeper of a vast cauldron of inspiration, called *Awen* in the Welsh. In this Cauldron – the same magical vessel described in the poem *the spoils of Annwfn* and symbolising the womb or heart of the land – is brewed a magical potion which bestows divine inspiration upon those who partake of its magic. This divine inspiration is not merely the ability to generate ideas, rather it is to become in-spirited – to attain the knowledge of all things, of all creation via a merging with the goddess. As such the ability to weave magic, shapeshift into various animals and objects and divine the future and the past all becomes possible.

When taken in the context of the Wildman or Wyllt, Awen or divine inspiration also comes as a result of this communion with the goddess, in this case embodied by the land itself. Complete immersion in nature aligns and bonds them utterly with the sovereignty and soul of the land, via access to Annwfn, the spirit world, for wisdom and renewal. Such a process is naturally mediated by Gwyn as its guardian, allowing access to the goddess and/or her sacred vessel only to those who are worthy of the honour.

Druids and bardic seekers have always used an immersion in either nature or darkness to seek wisdom. Time spent in retreat in wild places to get closer to the gods, sleeping by rivers and using the sounds of nature such as running water, or the movement of wind and clouds for divination- known as *neldoracht* are ancient practices. Enclosing oneself in a darkened hut under either a cloak, animal hide or with the palm of one's hands over one's eyes are also well documented druidic practice- known in the Irish lore as *Imbas Forosnai*. Similarly, in the writing of Taliesin we see references to being chained in the earth as an initiatory technique, possibly by sleeping in or burying oneself in the earth of a Neolithic burial or barrow mound –often known in the Welsh lore as "Ceriddwen's court" the 'hollow hills' of the Celtic Faery lore.

Therefore, in the tale of Gwyn and Cyledr we see an initiatory process afoot under the guise of grisly vengeance – by consuming his ancestral power Cyledr breaks down his mortal self and is able to access a deeper level of reality where connection to the divine becomes possible. Such initiations have always been considered dangerous and even undesirable if they come upon a soul unwillingly – it is certainly not an easy or pleasant process – but to undergo such a journey was considered to have rewards in the ability to commune with the gods and spirits, and access a wisdom and power unavailable to the average person. Such characters were sometimes able to bring these gifts back to the human everyday world for healing and renewal of the whole community. We do not see this end result with regards to Cyledr, and have no means of knowing whether he emerged from the process in the original full tale, but with the characters of Merlin and Taliesin we see these initiates can become mediators and travellers between the mortal world and Annwfn, accessing divine wisdom for the benefit of the mortal world.

Practice: Meeting the Wild Man

Seeking oracular enlightenment, the Awen, from an intimate immersive connection with nature is an ancient and perennial source of wisdom, allowing us to gradually connect with the deeper parts of ourselves and discover we are and have always been intricately bound to the rest of creation and the spirit world. Spending as much time in nature as possible is central to this process, not always an easy thing in the modern world – experiencing for yourself how your consciousness shifts after extended exposure to the land away from the trappings of civilisation is a great teacher in and of itself. It is within this wild isolation that we may most easily become aware of Gwyn and a host of unseen presences upon the land. After a matter of hours our relationship to our bodies as well as to our sense of identity begins to shift, diminishing our stress and external concerns and making us more present and 'grounded'. In such an environment, our ability to heed our inner voice and even begin to work with our inner eye and develop our seership becomes far easier. After longer periods the ability to connect with the land and even merge our consciousness with it begins to happen quite smoothly and gently, especially if we seek and encourage such a communion with the land and its spirit inhabitants within ourselves.

When sitting out deep in nature, try this simple invocation and visionary exercise to seek communion with the Wild Man's spirit.

First make an offering of song or milk to the land. In several places in Scotland they have what's called "Gruagach stones" – cup marked stones used for just this purpose. Choose somewhere that feels especially still and wild, and lay your gift upon the earth before retreating to somewhere suitably sheltered but nearby for you to meditate and commune.

Feeling your feet firmly on the ground, preferably barefoot, take several deep slow breaths. Really smell the air, the smell of the soil, of the green leaves, the smell of water or rain in the air itself. What scents come to you on the wind, what textures can you feel against your skin?

Now let your attention turn to within, to your heartbeat and the breath in your lungs. Feel the slow steady rhythm of life within you. Take your time and stay with this awhile, before calling out loud to encounter the spirit of the Wild man. Such figures may come to you from myth and legend or they may be the spirit guardian of the place in which you now sit, don't over analyse but let the experience unfold as it will.

Try these words or use your own:

"Spirit of the wild man, the divine Wyllt, I seek you in this wild place, let me feel your presence and your wisdom."

Keep your attention present to the earth beneath and around you and the blood and air within you, and approach the experience in a state of patient acceptance, be open to the Wild Man coming to you as he will, be it in a vision, a series of ideas and thoughts, a felt presence or something else.

They key to this exercise is patience and practice, being immersed in nature as much as possible and being sensitive to the slow subtle shifts of consciousness and presence that can occur.

Chapter 5

GWYN AND THE WILD HUNT
GWYN AND THE DEAD

Ages ago as a man who had been engaged on business, not the most creditable in the world, was returning in the depth of night across Cefn Creini, and thinking in a downcast frame of mind over what he had been doing, he heard in the distance a low and fear inspiring bark; and then another bark, and then another, and then half a dozen and more. Ere long he became aware that he was being pursued by dogs, and that they were *Cŵn Annwfn*. He beheld them coming, he tried to flee but he felt quite powerless and could not escape. Nearer and nearer they came, and he saw the shepherd with them: his face was black and he had horns on his head.[12]

As guardian of the underworld, Annwfn, Gwyn is said to be the leader of the Wild Hunt, a spectral hunt of hell or faery hounds, known in the Welsh as the *Cŵn Annwfn*. Tearing across the sky in the winter months, it brings terror across the land sweeping away the spirits of the dead. The hunt consists of a vast array of mounted hunters, demonic figures, faery beings and the dead themselves in a huge procession. In Wales, it is said to be an omen of death and has the curious property of sounding louder the further away it is. Sometimes its cries were said to be the wails of un-baptised children who were denied entrance to heaven.

The Wild Hunt is a pan-European tradition, in Northern Europe it is led by Odin or Woden, in the UK by numerous figures such as Woden, King Herla and Herne the Hunter but in Wales the leader of the hunt is always Gwyn, or that other mysterious lord of Annwfn, Arawn, who is most likely Gwyn by another name. In Norse lore, the Wild Hunt takes away the spirits of the dead, but it is also joined by various magical practitioners who may travel with it in spirit returning to their bodies unharmed. The Wild Hunt functions as a vast energetic wave sweeping across the land clearing away the dead and any unwelcome spirits, although it is also a subject of fear as an example of chthonic forces literally upending the normal structure and riding either across the land or in the sky bringing change, retribution for misdeeds or general chaos to the mortal world. Rather like the tarot card, The Tower, it represents an unavoidable current of change sweeping away the status quo. This is understandably disturbing, but taken from a wider perspective it can be understood as a natural function in the cycle of life, clearing the way for new life ahead. Its presence over the winter months points to this, as does its connections to storms and other moments of elemental, local or national crisis such as those referred to in the earliest written record of the Wild Hunt in Britain in Peterborough, apparently in reaction to the installation of a new Bishop. Recorded in the Anglo-Saxon Chronicles in 1127:

> ...it was seen and heard by many men: many hunters riding. The hunters were black, and great and loathy, and their hounds all black, and wide-eyed and loathy, and they rode on black horses and black he-goats. This was seen in the very deer park in the town of Peterborough, and in all the woods from the same town to Stamford; and the monks heard the horn blowing that they blew that night. Truthful men who kept watch at night said that it seemed to them that there might be about twenty or thirty horn blowers. This was seen and heard ... all through Lenten tide until Easter.[13]

To see the Hunt, or to have its presence noted in a community traditionally means that either a death is near or some injustice has taken place, especially in relation to leaders and leadership of an area – suggesting some link to the idea of sovereignty. The idea that the sanctity of the land or the nation is seen in some way as an entity whose well-being can be defended and vengeance taken upon transgressors goes beyond Christian teaching and taps in to something more primal and immediate. The fearsome reputation of the Wild Hunt through Christian times no doubt reflected a far greater fear of the dead and the underworld than it may have had in the distant past. Fear of the underworld or inner realms generally – be it a pagan underworld of which lingering evidence would have remained in folklore and in ancient sites such as barrow mounds and stone circles – or other states of inner power – women's bodies, sexual energies and people's own connections to their own soul and inner workings was now either denied, or placed firmly in the hands of the Clergy. To hear the Hunt pass by must have rocked the contained and constrained status quo of a community both religiously and psychologically – any force other than God and his angels roaming the land would surely point to the presence of demons or shake the validity of the whole Christian hegemony.

Ned Pugh's farewell

The faeries, and the Wild Hunt's love of music is well attested in folklore, with faeries regularly drawing musicians of all kinds into Annwfn. Sometimes such musicians return years later with even greater skill, while others are never seen again, or seem to become faeries themselves. One such tale is that of Ned Pugh, a fiddle player of great renown, who was said to have disappeared whilst exploring a cave at a place known at the time as Ness Cliff (now Nesscliff) near Shrewsbury. As he wandered into the hill he was heard playing his last tune, known as *Ned Pugh's Farewell*. The *Cambrian Quarterly Magazine* of 1829 tells a similar tale, giving him the name Iolo Ap Huw and recounting how he walked into the mist, all the time playing his fiddle and was never seen again until Halloween/Nos Calan Gaeaf, when he was witnessed cheering on the Cŵn Annwfn as part of the Wild Hunt, chasing madly over Cader Idris in Snowdonia. He had exchanged his fiddle for a bugle and was now huntsman in chief to Gwyn ap Nudd himself.

Practice: Call to the Wild Hunt

This rite can be used to seek the support of the Wild Hunt in matters of local or national concern. It is not suitable for petitioning the Hunt on personal matters, more to request their assistance in matters of leadership, protection and just rule of the people and the land on a wider scale. The Hunt cannot be bound or controlled and so cannot be forced into helping you, but if asked respectfully they may help in a way they decide if they consider the request to be just and the need genuine.

This is best performed at night on either dark of the moon, to bring change or full moon to call in strong positive leadership and protection for the land. However, the waning moon could also be used in times of great and obvious tyranny when something needs to be banished – but take special care with your words when seeking a banishing on a national or local scale because a greater picture may reveal something we're unaware of personally. Be sure to ask for a positive remedy, as they see fit, rather than presume you know the solution yourself. The result will be beyond your control. In this way, we are asking the guardians of the land to intervene as they see best, not attempting to dominate forces beyond our knowledge.

First clear your mind and consider the matter that concerns you carefully from all sides. See if you can be as clear as possible about the source of the problem without anger or prejudice clouding your vision. Knowing your own shadow is important here. See if you can write down a simple statement and request for what you seek. Re-write it as often as necessary until you feel you are precise and honest in what you say. For example:

"Lord of the Wild Hunt, wild ones of the Cŵn Annwfn, with respect please hear my petition. The land is wracked with pollution, the trees are felled for money and greed. We have lost our way. Please protect our land and know that not all our hearts are poisoned in this way. May there be healing and renewal between us and the land. Bring us wise ones and leaders who shall halt this destruction, and bring peace and health hereafter!"

Know that you are calling on one of the great primal forces of the land, and that if they decide to act it shall be in a manner and at a time entirely of their choosing not yours. The call to bring peace after, and the important point of leaving out any words that call for violence or vengeance are for your good conscience and show them that you are trying to be of good true heart in the matter even if your feelings are strong and the peril is great. This may or may not make your petition more successful, but it keeps your energy field clear.

Next prepare an offering – see the section on faery offerings, but know that in this instance some meat or good alcohol like mead or whiskey may feel the most suitable. Again, you must think on it carefully and make your own decision, listening to your inner voice and intuition. You may wish to visit the Wild Hunt in vision or in a shamanic journey to discover what offering they would like.

Then you will need to prepare a lantern that can burn safely outside and clear and tidy your space. This rite is best performed outside so make that area as pleasant, well-ordered and sacred as you can, taking practicalities into consideration.

Cast a circle and/or call in your guardians and allies to assist you, and then in your own words call upon Gwyn and the Wild Hunt. It's best to speak for yourself but if you're uncertain try this or something like it:

"Gwyn ap Nudd, bright one in the darkness, lord of the hunt, I call to you! I call to the Wild Hunt, forces of Annwfn to hear my plea!"

Place your offering down on the ground, or on your altar, table etc., depending on your space, and make it clear this gift is for them. For example:

71

"My Lord Gwyn and your fierce hounds please accept this gift, as a sign of my thanks and respect."

If it is an offering of meat, you may wish to add:

"May this be the only blood spilled this day!"

Next take the lantern and light it, holding it up to the skies and say this or your own words:

"In the ways of the people from the earliest days, may this lantern guide your way!"

Place the lantern next to the offering, and silently call them again to you, breathing deeply.

You may feel a shift and change in the atmosphere, you may hear the call of a night bird, or the bark of a dog or none of this may happen; if there is silence it doesn't mean they won't hear you. Their behaviour and motives are outside your control or your mortal understanding. The best you can do is approach it honestly and with a brave clear heart. When you are ready, read out aloud your petition. You may wish to repeat it several times, or even many times over and over building power with each recital like a conventional spoken spell, again you will have to feel for yourself how many times and how you should say it, quietly, loudly, rhythmically etc.

When you are finished hold your arms up to the sky and thank Gwyn and the Hunt for hearing you, and bow once, to be sure you've shown your respect. Place the petition next to the offering and the lantern, and bury it the next day, or burn it in the candle flame straight away as you feel.

Finish by thanking your guides and allies and/or closing your circle if you cast one, and return indoors. Don't go back out that night but clear up your offering and the lantern the next day.

The dialogue of Gwyddno Garanhir and Gwyn ap Nudd[14]

Recorded in the Black Book of Carmarthen, dated to 1250CE, *The Dialogue of Gwyddno Garanhir and Gwyn ap Nudd* is the earliest surviving manuscript written completely in Welsh. The Black Book is a collection of ninth to twelfth- century poetry and triads – collections of lore and mythology gathered in threes and much of the poetry, especially the *dialogue,* is written in the form of a series of englinion, a traditional poetic form consisting of three-line stanzas with a fixed number of syllables.

The dialogue consists at the beginning of a typical exchange of each party speaking in turn, appearing at first to be a defeated warrior seeking protection from his victorious attacker in battle. However, as the poem develops this form breaks down into a longer monologue from Gwyn ap Nudd and we can see that something else is happening here. Gradually it becomes clearer that this is a conversation between a fallen warrior and Gwyn as the figure of death or psychopomp leading the fallen to Annwfn.

Much of the early Welsh verses are notoriously difficult to translate and obscure in their references, often being scraps of a far larger body of work now lost. The most easily available translation of the dialogue is by W. F. Skene, in 1868 and few quality translations have been made since, the most notable of which is by Jenny Rowland (1990)[15], however, much of her version diverges from Skene's only in minor details, other than in the latter half which she separates entirely from the main body of the text in the belief that it is in fact a separate poem entirely. For this reason, I have decided here to work through Skene's text, pointing out differences and debate in the meaning as they arise.

Gwyddno Garanhir whose name means 'Tall crane' was said to have been the king of the sunken kingdom of Cantre'r Gwaelod in what is now Cardigan Bay on the Welsh coast. He was the father of Elffin the foster father of divine poet Taliesin, and his position as a king of a kingdom now under the sea, together with his name – cranes are often associated with the otherworld as beings of air and water – hint at his own otherworldly nature and possible connection to Annwfn, so often accessed over water.

The Dialogue begins with Gwyddno seeking protection from Gwyn, presumably after battle, praising Gwyn and his honourable behaviour in bestowing his protection.

> Bull of conflict was he, active in dispersing an arrayed army,
> The ruler of hosts, indisposed to anger,
> Blameless and pure his conduct in protecting life.

He is then answered by Gwyn.
Against a hero stout was his advance,
The ruler of hosts, disposer of wrath.
There will be protection for thee since thou askest it.

Gwyddno then replies:

For thou hast given me protection;
How warmly wert though welcomed!
The hero of hosts from what region thou comest?

He is answered that Gwyn comes fresh from the battle. Here
Rowland's text differs from Skene's making it clearer that Gwyn
has been at the battle but not fallen victim himself.

I come from battle and conflict
With a shield in my hand;
Broken is the helmet by the pushing of spears.
Or in Rowland's translation:
I come from battle and great hewing
With shield in hand
Spear blows shattered heads.[16]

So Gwyddno replies:

I will address thee, exalted man,
With this shield in distress; (here Rowland gives it as '*shield in*
battle')[17]
Brave man, what is thy descent?

And Gwyn answers:

Hound-hoofed is my horse, the torment of battle, (here Rowland
gives the horses name as *Carngrwn* – rather than '*hound hoofed*')[18]

75

Whilst I am called Gwyn, the son of Nud,
The lover of Creudilad, the daughter of Llud.

And Gwyddno names himself:

Since it is thou, Gwyn, an upright mau, (Rowland – *'a true warrior'*)[19]
From thee there is no concealing;
I also am Gwydneu Garanhir.

Here Gwyn refers to his horse who is eager to be away:

He will not leave me in a parley with thee,
By the bridle, as is becoming;
But will hasten away to his home on the Tawy.

And Gwyddno replies:

It is not the nearest Tawy I speak of to thee,
But the furthest Tawy
Eagle! I will cause the furious sea to ebb. (here Rowlands translates as *'by the shore of the sea, a fierce ebbing'*.[20] (This is interesting, that there are two Tawys being discussed, perhaps being the same place but in the spirit realm of Annwfn and the mortal world simultaneously, revealed when the otherworldly waters ebb or recede.)

The next two englynion are Gwyn's. Caer Vandwy features as an otherworldly destination in Annwfn and this next section could refer to his part in defending Annwfn in the famous raid by Arthur, attested in Taliesin's poem 'Preiddeu Annwfn' 'The spoils of Annwn', discussed earlier.

Polished is my ring, golden my saddle and bright
To my sadness

I saw a conflict before Caer Vandwy.

Before Caer Vandwy a host I saw,
Shields were shattered and ribs broken
Renowned and splendid was he who made the assault.

Here Gwyddno interrupts:

Gwyn ab Nud, the hope (Rowland – *benefit*) of armies,
Sooner would legions fall before the hoofs
Of thy horses, than broken rushes to the ground.
And Gwyn continues, referring to his faery hound, and chief
ally Dormach. (Dormach – "death's door".)
Handsome (Rowland – *Beautiful*) my dog and round-bodied,
(Rowland – *fair*)[21]
And truly the best of dogs;
Dormach was he, which belonged to Maelgwyn.
Dormach with the ruddy nose! what a gazer
Thou art upon me! because I notice
Thy wanderings on Gwibir Vynyd. (Rowland – *'above on the sky'*.[22]
Here we see Gwyn and his hound's role in the wild hunt, racing
across the sky becomes apparent.)

Here the englynion shift into a monologue from Gwyn, and some
scholars including Rowland argue that this is a separate poem
entirely, but this is far from clear. That it goes on to list a role of
deeds where Gwyn, as death or psychopomp has seen the passing
of warriors makes it connect smoothly with the previous englynion
even if only as an addendum.

I have been in the place where was killed Gwendoleu,
The son of Ceidaw, the pillar of songs,
When the ravens screamed over blood.

I have been in the place where Bran was killed,
The son of Gweryd, of far-extending fame,
When the ravens of the battle-field screamed.

I have been where Llachau was slain,
The son of Arthur, extolled in songs,
When the ravens screamed over blood.

I have been where Meurig was killed,
The son of Carreian, of honourable fame,
When the ravens screamed over flesh.

I have not (Have I not?) been where Gwallawg was killed,
The son of Goholeth, the accomplished,
The resister of Lloegir, the son of Lleynawg.

I have been where the soldiers of Prydain were slain,
From the East to the North;
I am alive, they in their graves!

I have been where the soldiers of Prydain were slain,
From the East to the South
I am alive, they in death![23]

The dialogue presents us with interesting clues to Gwyn's role as psychopomp and facilitator of the dead, a role which can be seen in his hunting of the Boar Trwch in the tale of Culhwch and Olwen and which he retains in later folklore as leader of the Wild Hunt. Here we see Gwyn's own words and experience depicted for the first and only time, ever on the move visiting battle after battle and active in his guardianship over Annwfn as well as in the mortal world, with his faithful hound, Dormach, "death's door".

The figure of death, or leader of the Wild Hunt is one usually treated as something to fear, and in the later folklore the Wild

Hunt is seen as chasing demons across the skies, and Gwyn is described as holding demons within him as he controls or oversees their containment. Yet we can see the overt Christianisation of this aspect of the tradition here, as his task is the gathering up of fallen warriors not demons, and much is made of his granting his 'protection' to Gwyddno, ensuring his safe passage from one world to the next. Gwyn is described as 'exalted' and the 'benefit' of armies. When we consider what it is to be the guardian of Annwfn, even one in the Christian view as filled with demons, it is clear that such a being would be noted for their mercy and be 'holy', as Gwyn's name suggests, rather than a cursed jailer. This is a sacred role, for one who sees no soul lost and wandering, a trusted guide and protector through otherworldly journeys and transitions. The ancient Celts famously held no fear of death and believed in reincarnation; that they cycled through the worlds, life after life, a system beautifully symbolised in the triple spiral – and that the descent into the underworld was nothing to fear. Rather by the guardian's protection you would be held and guided on your way when your time came.

There are many psychopomp figures in world mythology and religions, from Hermes and Anubis through to the Norse Valkyries and the Archangel Michael. The term comes from the Greek words *psyche* (breath, life, soul) and *pompos* (conductor or guide), literally to guide or escort the soul on its journey. Such a role often has its human mortal counterparts on this side of the veil and the work of soul leading has been undertaken by cultures all around the world, usually performed by priests or priestesses especially trained for the task, or other practitioners such as shaman and wise women, preparing both body and soul for the transition, and handing over the spirit of the deceased to forces on the other side when the time comes. Such roles are usually undertaken with immense respect and compassion for the soul and all the surrounding family members and is not undertaken lightly.

Soul leading

Soul leading or soul midwifery is a sacred task, and too vast and serious a subject to cover here in any suitable depth from a practitioner's point of view. To guide and prepare someone for their death is something profoundly intimate and deserves an astounding level of compassion and sensitivity, where a spiritual view needs psychological and practical skills alongside to be of genuine service.

In the modern era we tend to distance ourselves from and fear death, yet it is something we all will experience – none of us will escape the death of a loved one or our own passing, and to gently prepare ourselves for this eventuality can begin to shift this sense of taboo within our own psyches at least and help to guide us in our final moments and in our journey beyond. Easing our fear and helping us to access something greater within ourselves when the time comes, a sense of surrender and even courage perhaps.

In the Celtic tradition, the transition of the spirit or soul after death is overseen by numerous guides and protectors as well as Gwyn, such as the Three Mothers, or Dea Matronae, which we know of from numerous inscriptions and reliefs found across Northern Europe from the first to fifth centuries CE. These depict three women of indeterminate age, although young and older married women may be referred to via the style of dress. These women, or 'mothers' oversee all stages of life and death, childbirth and rearing as well as the laying out of the dead and their journey to the underworld. Traces of them can be seen in the myths of the Morrigan who may sometimes have a triple form, as well as figures from folklore such as *'the washer at the ford'* – a spectral faery woman seen washing funeral shrouds in the river – and a common omen of death. These female deities hold and support the spirit of the departed in their transformation, just as a mother holds her newborn baby after its arrival in our mortal world. This is symbolised by the enduring image of the cauldron of Annwfn, the great womb both receiving and giving out life in endless cycles, of which Gwyn is the primary protector ensuring only the worthy get to access the power of her sacred vessel, and seeing that no spirit is lost upon the journey.

Space clearing and soul blessing

Sometimes the spirits of the dead resist the journey to the underworld, for numerous reasons, and these may require our attention in order to restore peace to all. Sometimes the deeds of their lives have tied them karmically to specific places and people, or they feel they have unfinished business or desires that tie them to the mortal world. Sometimes it is their loved ones who hold on so tight the departed spirit does not feel free to leave. Such spirit presences may remain largely positive and keep a lot of their previous personality, while others become increasingly negative and lacking in coherent consciousness over time. On other occasions mere energetic patterns may remain, like a stain or an indentation on the fabric of the world. In such cases the spirit doesn't remain, but its imprint was so strong – usually due to emotional strain or shock – that others may see it as a ghost that repeats the same movement, sound or gesture over and over like a recording. At other times, the traces of their lives can linger on in their bloodline, where those that come after are tied to repeating the same mistakes or energetic patterns, such as illness, bad luck, and emotional betrayal, until the pattern is released, most often by shamanic ancestral healing. More rarely, other types of spirit linger to disturb the mortal world and those within it, and these too need to be dealt with for their own good as much as anyone else's. Thankfully the established protocols for this are clear.

When considering the souls of the dead, whether the newly departed or those of the distant past, the key rule is to remember compassion, and to call in greater assistance to help us. The deeds of their lives are now over and in the past, and the soul is deserving of compassion and kindness without judgement, the purity of their state should be remembered even if the spirits themselves do not express this yet or have undergone that process. This may be difficult, but it is not our job alone to help lost spirits, rather we must keep a clear line between the living and the dead and call upon Gwyn and other helpers, especially ancestral allies to use their skill and compassion to assist. It is rather the power of our care, and of our asking for assistance for them, that re-connects them with the great web of life between the worlds and facilitates their release, guiding them on to the next stage in the process.

Practice: Space cleansing

Try this simple prayer to Gwyn or create your own to call in his assistance if you feel a space or home is inhabited by a trapped or lost spirit, of any kind.

"Great Gwyn ap Nudd, blessed one, shining one, come to our assistance here!

Bring your great light and shine it throughout this house,

I feel there is a presence here who has lingered beyond their time,

send us your protection!

And guide this lost soul onwards to Annwfn, and to their rest!"

Should you need greater protection you may add or create your own prayer with this is mind.

This one for example calls upon Gwyn as he is portrayed in the Dialogue of Gwyn and Gwyddno Garanhir, and also calls upon the assistance of Gwyn's hound, Dormach of the ruddy nose, chief dog of the Cŵn Annwfn. Hounds and dogs are often called upon to clear away dead energy and the spirits of the dead, and are faithful spirit allies as well as strong guardian spirits in their own right.

"Gwyn ap Nudd, Hope of Armies, come to my aid, be my shield and protector!

Clear the home and hearth of my enemies and the spirits of those who would wish me ill!

Dormach hound, chase these uninvited spirits from this house and leave peace in your wake!

Gwyn Bright Lord, scour the land that only goodness may reside here!"

In both cases, leaving an offering of thanks for Gwyn and his faery hunt is advised, such as a gift of honey or mead, or something you have made of your own hands.

Should you wish to create a sacred space or circle for this work, using a Blackthorn wand is most advised in the case of hostile spirits, or using Aspen to assist in opening the door between the worlds and ease their passage is a traditional wood for entrance to the underworld and negotiating between the dead and the living.

Practice: Saining

The Scots Gaelic tradition of *Saining* can be used as well to help clear or bless a space before or after any of this work. Similar to the Native American tradition of 'smudging' using sage, here we use juniper smoke to clear and bless. Juniper can be cast upon a fire, burnt in bundles like sage or burnt upon a charcoal brick. Always take care to be safe, juniper may spit hot sparks. You may like to waft the smoke around your home using your hand or a feather. Always thank the spirit of the juniper for their work and continue to ask the good spirits to assist you.

Use your own words or try these, as you sain your home:

"Spirit of the juniper, bless and cleanse this space, I thank you green ally! Bring peace and goodness here! With our blessings and thanks!"

Practice: Ancestral guidance

In this meditation journey, we will seek the council of our ancient ancestors, and seek a primary ancestral guide to advise you when your time in the mortal world is done, one who will come to meet you as you cross the mists to Annwfn.

This exercise is best performed somewhere quiet where you are comfortable but will remain uninterrupted for at least half an hour.

First sitting upright, close your eyes and take three deep

breaths. Call to your guides and spiritual allies, whether you know them by name or not – trust that they attend you, then state your intention out loud to seek an encounter with a guide and those of your bloodline from the distant past. Neither you nor they need to have been Welsh or British or Celtic at all, nor need they have to come from the land on which you now dwell, wherever that may be. Trust the wisdom of the spirits to bring you the right guide, who knows your path truly.

In your inner vision see yourself standing at a great stone archway with a path of pale stone stretching out ahead of you. The path leads across a wide plain of gently swaying grass. When you are ready, step through the stone archway and follow the path. It leads you through the grassland and to a place where the ground grows marshy and reeds grow tall. The path turns to a trackway of wood leading out to the edge of a great expanse of water. Notice what you see and hear, and what you feel. Notice the colour of the sky overhead.

As you approach the water's edge, still standing on the trackway, you see a small boat comes to you across the water. A hooded figure stands in the prow to meet you. As they draw closer they hold out their hand to guide you onto the boat. They may have a message for you or they may say nothing, as the two of you sail across the waters. Ahead you see a land of green rolling hills and distant mountains.

When you come to the opposite shore you are met by your ancestral guide, one of your distant bloodline. They may take any form, and they may or may not have messages for you. Thank the boatman and go with your guide. In time, they lead you up into the hills behind them.

You walk with them through the green land of rolling fields and up into the hills. Eventually you see the entrance to a cave ahead of you, with a broad open entrance, and flickering light within. Your guide leads you inside and you see a great fire with all manner of people sat around it. Some sing and drum and dance. Others sit quietly. Some are busy making things or mending things, others hold children, or sleep peacefully.

Your guide signals you to take your place among them for a while. Some may approach you, and you may go and speak with whoever you wish. Your guide will advise you if necessary. Spend time here with your ancestors in Annwfn.

When it is time to leave, your guide signals for you to say farewell and you return the way you came. Thank your guide for their assistance. They lead you to the boat but remain upon the shore as you sail across the waters back to the reeds and the wooden trackway. Follow the path back through the grass and feel the breath in your lungs, the blood in your veins leading you back to your body.

Cross through the stone archway and feel yourself fully returned – back in your body gently and easily.

Feel the breath in your chest, and breathe in and out a few times, and wiggle your fingers and toes to feel yourself back firmly in your body. You may like to record your experiences in a journal.

Afterwards you may like to have a pillar candle which you can light to honour and remember your ancestors and your ancestral guide from time to time.

Practice: Ancestral prayers

Should you suspect there is trouble in your family bloodline, unfinished business or repeated patterns, you may call upon Gwyn ap Nudd to help heal and resolve these issues.

First set up an ancestral altar – this can be as elaborate or as simple as you choose and can include the recently passed as well as those who lived thousands of years ago if you wish. Place upon it photos or any objects which remind you or may represent your ancestors to you, including photos of places and even soil or stone from your homeland or places where some of your roots reside. You could even place a mirror there, so that you can look into your own face and remember those whose DNA have contributed to your presence here and your own features.

Next regularly place simple offerings to your ancestors there, such as burning a little incense, fresh flowers, or the odd cup of tea; whatever feels right for you. Accompany your offerings with a small prayer to them and to Gwyn to assist in their healing.

You may like to try this one:

"Ancestors, my grandparents and theirs, and theirs back to the beginning! I call to you! Gwyn ap Nudd, lord of Annwfn I call to you! Help me remember those of my blood, and send them healing and love! Your good deeds live on, and your failings are forgiven, dissolved in the great cauldron of the goddess! Know that you are free and honoured! May Gwyn ap Nudd guide you to rest and peace! May his shining light make a path for you through the darkness! May those of our line who know the journey step forward to meet and guide you! May you know yourselves renewed! Peace! Peace! Peace upon you!"

Conclusion

GWYN AND The CAULDRON INITIATION

Gwyn oversees and guards a most sacred process and journey for the soul, one that can be performed many times over in a mortal life, on whichever land or in whatever era we live, and will be repeated again to a deeper level upon our deaths – namely the return to the cauldron; the womb and tomb of the goddess where we will find inspiration and renewal each in its due season.

To walk this path means that we must walk in harmony with the cycles and rhythms of the earth as much as possible. Time spent in nature is irreplaceable; time venerating our sacred sites and most ancient trees and springs as places where the veil thins, where the mist between the worlds gathers, means that the energies of the land and its spirit inhabitants are able to work their own magic upon us, to nurture our soul's evolution and help us re-remember the old ways with their prompting. What we have today is broken fragments of forgotten lore to guide us and tempt us further into the mists, but we must remember to not let our analytical thinking tell us that either we have found all the answers, nor that the task is too large for us to ever feel our way along the path ahead. The old tales and poems were deliberately obscure, our ancient oracular bards deliberately revelled in a multiplicity of meanings, so that each audience could unpick them and see them with fresh eyes over and over, like gazing into the depths of the cauldron itself. We must trust ourselves as adventurers and trust a little to the spirits and the gods themselves, for they have never forgotten and will show us if we approach them in the right way.

In this final practice, we will seek nourishment from the cauldron itself by returning to meet Gwyn and the faery court, but only once the correct etiquette has been performed and we have proven ourselves worthy. This final journey for vision should only be undertaken when we have spent much time meditating out in nature and made offerings to the Tylwyth Teg, and journeyed to meet Gwyn many times. Similarly, we should also have journeyed to meet Gwythyr and Creiddylad more than once. It should also only be performed once we have come to know ourselves as much

as we can for a while, when we are already mature on our path of self-knowledge, and have sought our reflection in the dark mirror journey.

Start this meditation by creating a sacred space in whichever way you choose, and taking three deep breaths to calm and centre yourself. In your own way call any guides or allies to you that you may choose to work with, and aloud or in your own mind state your intention to encounter Gwyn ap Nudd the chief of Annwfn, lord of faery. Try this meditation in the wild lonely places of forest or hillside if you can, or beside a river, but wherever you do it, be sure the place will be peaceful so that your inner vision is not disturbed.

Feel your feet steady on the ground beneath you, and the breath slow and steady in your lungs. In your inner eye see your feet standing on soft earth, a beaten path across a grassy meadow. Ahead of you see a vast green hill stretching up into the sky. Its sides are clothed with dense forest and the air above it shimmers with many colours as if bursts of magical fire are emanating from its summit.

You follow the path across the meadow and see it leads you into a gap in the trees. As soon as you step under the leafy canopy you sense a shift in atmosphere. This is a sacred place, it's as if the trees hide something from sight, and you hear the sound of hooves on soft earth but see nothing. The path pale against the shadows of the trees upon the ground guides you in a wide arc around the hill, and disappears out of sight in a large spiral. Concentrate on your footsteps, one step after another, and feel the cool air on your cheek and the silent presence of the trees all around.

Eventually your path grows steeper and rockier, and up ahead you see the path terminates not on the summit, but at a small cavern entrance in the side of the hill. A hawthorn tree curls around it and the air is filled with its heady perfume. At the foot of this tree you see a figure sits, calm and still. You cannot see their face, but your skin tingles at the feeling of power all around you in this quiet place.

Walk up to the figure by the entrance, and bow. Greet them politely. They stand and ask you your reason for being here. Answer them honestly, with the first words that rise from your heart. If the guardian is satisfied you may enter the cavern. Remember this is sacred ground, with every step you draw closer to the heart of the earth. The guardian comes with you to assist you with etiquette and can be called upon for advice and guidance to this realm should you need it.

Inside you see you are standing at the beginning of a tunnel. The walls are lined with crystal veins and shimmer in the light of torches. There is a cord of twisted rope guiding you down into the hill. Down the tunnel you go, holding your intention clear in your heart to encounter the faery court.

All at once the tunnel ends and you find yourself in a vast cavern lined with crystal and the deep roots of trees.

You have been here before but this time you see the place with fresh eyes. Ahead, a pool of water is fed from two small springs emerging from the rock. All around you is the faery host.

They take a myriad of forms, and some of them shift and change and shimmer as you look at them. They may take the forms of animals, trees, shadow and sparkling light, shifting in and out of humanoid form in the blink of an eye. Others are more settled and human in their appearance, and regard you with cool, stern eyes, or even mockery. Some smile and greet you kindly. There are others there, ancient ancestors and faery travellers recently passed.

Across the hall are two thrones. On one throne sits a tall figure with long dark hair. Light radiates from him, dazzling and shimmering. He looks down upon you with bright eyes.

This is Gwyn, lord of Annwfn.

The guardian leads you to the throne. Greet the lord of this realm with a bow and your honest words. Take three deep breaths and try to hold your consciousness here for a while that you may receive his wisdom. Give this plenty of time.

When Gwyn sees fit, he signals that you may turn and be led to his side, where his Queen is seated. You may have sought her long or had glimpses of her in vision, yet here she sits before you and as you gaze upon her all turns to dazzling light.

Let yourself be immersed in this light, let it fill every cell in your body, let it fill your eyes, your lungs and your heart until you breathe and see and feel only light.

Within this dazzling brightness you may be offered a sip from the cauldron, the lady may rise and speak with you or you may have your own vision from her. Let the light surround you and be all that you are, whatever else you experience. Breathe in and be one with this light, deep in the heart of the land herself. Stay here as long as you may, as long as you can.

Be blessed. Be renewed.

After a while you may return to a simpler vision, and be led by the guardian to return the way you came. Remember to thank the Lady, and honour her always.

Return the way you came, up through the tunnel and through the spiral path through the trees. As you emerge from the forest, take a moment to be aware of the change of light and feel your breath in your chest. As you walk, feel your body more and more until you come to the edge of the meadow and return completely to your everyday awareness.

Open your eyes and breathe deeply, feeling the air in your lungs hold you to the present time. Wriggle your fingers and toes, stamp your feet and take your time to feel fully grounded before perhaps recording your experiences in a journal or notebook.

You may return here whenever you choose, by the blessings of the lady.

May Gwyn ap Nudd guide your path.

NOTES

1. Lindahl,C., McNamara, J., Lindow, J. *Medieval Folklore: A guide to myths, legends, tales, beliefs, and customs,* Oxford University Press, 2002, p. 190
2. Davies, S. (trans.) *The Mabinogion,* Oxford, 2008, p. 199
3. Forest, D. 2017. Note that my translation whilst aiming to be as accurate as possible comes from a bardic as well as a linguistic perspective. For more academic translations see Haycock, M. 'Legendary poems from the book of Taliesin' 2015, Koch, J. 2003, 'The Heroic Age: Literary sources for ancient Celtic Europe and early Ireland and Wales.' and Higley, S. Camelot Project, 2007, http://d.lib.rochester.edu/camelot/text/preiddeu-annwn. (Accessed 30/6/17)
4. Spence, L. *The Faery Tradition in Britain,* Kessinger, p. 74
5. Sikes, W. *British Goblins,* 1973, p. 36
6. Crocker,C. *Fairy legends and traditions of the south of Ireland,* Vols 1-3. John Murray, 1915, p. 198
7. Guest, Lady C. *The Mabinogion,* Harper Collins, 2000, p. 260
8. The Life of Gildas, c. 1130-1150, stanza 14. http://sourcebooks.fordham.edu/halsall/basis/1150-Caradoc-LifeofGildas.asp (accessed 17/5/17)
9. Davies, S. (trans.) *The Mabinogion,* Oxford, 2008, p. 189
10. Lindahl, C. (ed.) and McNamara, J. (ed.) *Medieval folklore: an encyclopaedia of myths, legends, tales, beliefs, and customs,* Oxford University Press, 2002, p. 190
11. http://www.museum.ie/Archaeology/Exhibitions/Current-Exhibitions/Kingship-and-Sacrifice/Cashel-Man. (accessed 9/4/17)
12. J.H. Roberts in Edwards, *Cymru,* 1897, pp. 148-51
13. Westwood, J. and Simpson, J. Anglo-Saxon Chronicles. *The Lore of the Land,* Penguin, 2005, p. 393
14. Skene, W.F. (trans.) *The Black Book of Carmarthen XXXIII from*

The Four Ancient Books of Wales, 1868

15. Rowland, J., *Early Welsh saga poetry: A Study and Edition of the Englynion,* D.S. Brewer, 1990, p. 506-7
16. ibid.
17. ibid.
18. ibid.
19. ibid.
20. ibid.
21. ibid.
22. ibid.
23. Skene, W.F. (trans.) The Black Book of Carmarthen XXXIII from The Four Ancient Books of Wales, 1868

bibliography

Crocker, C., Fairy legends and traditions of the south of Ireland. Vols 1-3. (John Murray, 1915).

Davies. S., (trans.) The Mabinogion. (Oxford University Press. 2008).

Guest, Lady C., The Mabinogion. (Harper Collins, 2000).

Haycock. M., Legendary poems from the book of Taliesin. (Aberystwyth, 2015).

Koch. J., The Celtic Heroic Age: Literary sources for ancient Celtic Europe and early Ireland and Wales. (Celtic Studies Publications. 2003).

Lindahl. C, McNamara. J, Lindow. J, *Medieval Folklore: A guide to myths, legends, tales, beliefs, and customs.* (Oxford University Press. 2002,)

Roberts. J.H., in Edwards, *Cymru*, 1897.

Rowland, J., Early Welsh saga poetry: A Study and Edition of the Englynion. (D.S. Brewer,. 1990).

Sikes. W., British Goblins. 1880 (E.P. Publishing. 1973).

Skene, W.F., (trans.) The Black Book of Carmarthen XXXIII from The Four Ancient Books of Wales, 1868.

Spence. L., *The Faery Tradition in Britain*. (Kessinger. 1995).

Westwood. J., and Simpson. J., excerpt Anglo-Saxon Chronicles, found in *The Lore of the Land*. (Penguin, 2005).

Websites

Higley, S., Camelot Project,. 2007, http://d.lib.rochester.edu/camelot/text/preiddeu-annwn.

The Life of Gildas, Cc. 1130-1150, stanza 14. http://sourcebooks.fordham.edu/halsall/basis/1150-Caradoc-LifeofGildas.asp

http://www.museum.ie/Archaeology/Exhibitions/Current-Exhibitions/Kingship-and-Sacrifice/Cashel-Man.

We think you will also enjoy…

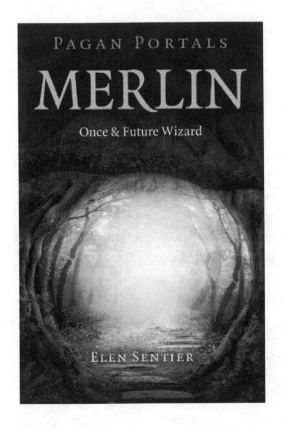

Merlin: Once and Future Wizard, Elen Sentier

Merlin in history, Merlin in mythology, Merlin through the ages and his
continuing relevance

*…a grand and imaginative work that introduces the reader to the many
faces of the mysterious Merlin.*
Morgan Daimler

978-1-78535-453-3 (paperback)
978-1-78535-454-0 (e-book)

Best Selling Pagan Portals & Shaman Pathways

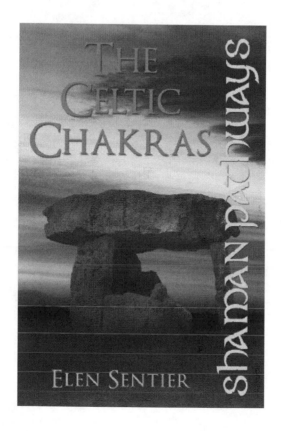

Celtic Chakras, Elen Sentier

Tread the British native shaman's path, explore the Goddess
hidden in the ancient stories; walk the Celtic chakra spiral
labyrinth.

Rich with personal vision, the book is an interesting exploration of
wholeness
Emma Restall Orr

978-1-78099-506-9 (paperback)
978-1-78099-507-6 (e-book)

Druid Shaman, Danu Forest

A practical guide to Celtic shamanism with exercises and techniques as well as traditional lore for exploring the Celtic Otherworld

A sound, practical introduction to a complex and wide-ranging subject
Philip Shallcrass

978-1-78099-615-8 (paperback)
978-1-78099-616-5 (e-book)

Kitchen Witchcraft, Rachel Patterson
Take a glimpse at the workings of a Kitchen Witch and share in
the crafts

*A wonderful little book which will get anyone started on Kitchen
Witchery. Informative, and easy to follow*
Janet Farrar & Gavin Bone

978-1-78099-843-5 (paperback)
978-1-78099-842-8 (e-book)

Moon Magic, Rachel Patterson

An introduction to working with the phases of the Moon

...a delightful treasury of lore and spiritual musings that should be essential to any planetary magic-worker's reading list.
David Salisbury

978-1-78279-281-9 (paperback)
978-1-78279-282-6 (e-book)

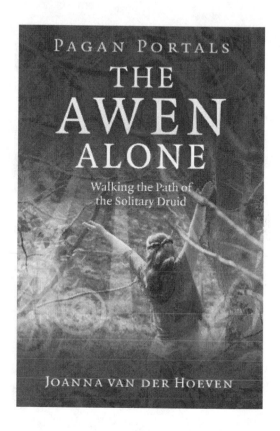

The Awen Alone, Joanna van der Hoeven
An introductory guide for the solitary Druid

Joanna's voice carries the impact and knowledge of the ancestors,
combined with the wisdom of contemporary understanding.
Cat Treadwell

978-1-78279-547-6 (paperback)
978-1-78279-546-9 (e-book)

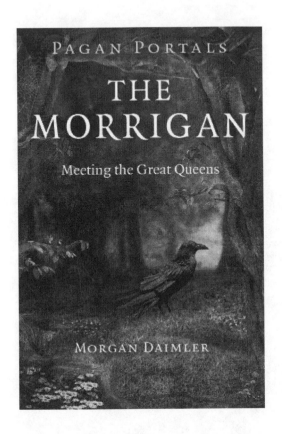

The Morrigan, Morgan Daimler

On shadowed wings and in raven's call, meet the ancient Irish
Goddess of war, battle, prophecy, death, sovereignty, and magic

*...a well-researched and heartfelt guide to the Morrigan from a fellow
devotee and priestess*
Stephanie Woodfield

978-1-78279-833-0 (paperback)
978-1-78279-834-7 (e-book)

Moon Books

PAGANISM & SHAMANISM

What is Paganism? A religion, a spirituality, an alternative belief
system, nature worship? You can find support for all these
definitions (and many more) in dictionaries, encyclopaedias, and
text books of religion, but subscribe to any one and the truth will
evade you. Above all Paganism is a creative pursuit, an encounter
with reality, an exploration of meaning and an expression of the
soul. Druids, Heathens, Wiccans and others, all contribute their
insights and literary riches to the Pagan tradition. Moon Books
invites you to begin or to deepen your own encounter, right here,
right now.
If you have enjoyed this book, why not tell other readers by
posting a review on your preferred book site.

Recent bestsellers from Moon Books are:

Journey to the Dark Goddess
How to Return to Your Soul
Jane Meredith
Discover the powerful secrets of the Dark Goddess and
transform your depression, grief and pain into healing
and integration.
Paperback: 978-1-84694-677-6 ebook: 978-1-78099-223-5

Shamanic Reiki
Expanded Ways of Working with Universal Life Force Energy
Llyn Roberts, Robert Levy
Shamanism and Reiki are each powerful ways of healing; together,
their power multiplies. *Shamanic Reiki* introduces techniques to
help healers and Reiki practitioners tap ancient healing wisdom.
Paperback: 978-1-84694-037-8 ebook: 978-1-84694-650-9

Pagan Portals – The Awen Alone
Walking the Path of the Solitary Druid
Joanna van der Hoeven
An introductory guide for the solitary Druid, *The Awen Alone* will
accompany you as you explore, and seek out your own place
within the natural world.
Paperback: 978-1-78279-547-6 ebook: 978-1-78279-546-9

A Kitchen Witch's World of Magical Herbs & Plants
Rachel Patterson
A journey into the magical world of herbs and plants, filled with
magical uses, folklore, history and practical magic. By popular
writer, blogger and kitchen witch, Tansy Firedragon.
Paperback: 978-1-78279-621-3 ebook: 978-1-78279-620-6

Medicine for the Soul
The Complete Book of Shamanic Healing
Ross Heaven
All you will ever need to know about shamanic healing and how to become your own shaman...
Paperback: 978-1-78099-419-2 ebook: 978-1-78099-420-8

Shaman Pathways – The Druid Shaman
Exploring the Celtic Otherworld
Danu Forest
A practical guide to Celtic shamanism with exercises and techniques as well as traditional lore for exploring the Celtic Otherworld.
Paperback: 978-1-78099-615-8 ebook: 978-1-78099-616-5

Traditional Witchcraft for the Woods and Forests
A Witch's Guide to the Woodland with Guided Meditations and Pathworking
Melusine Draco
A Witch's guide to walking alone in the woods, with guided meditations and pathworking.
Paperback: 978-1-84694-803-9 ebook: 978-1-84694-804-6

Wild Earth, Wild Soul
A Manual for an Ecstatic Culture
Bill Pfeiffer
Imagine a nature-based culture so alive and so connected, spreading like wildfire. This book is the first flame...
Paperback: 978-1-78099-187-0 ebook: 978-1-78099-188-7

Naming the Goddess
Trevor Greenfield

Naming the Goddess is written by over eighty adherents and scholars of Goddess and Goddess Spirituality.

Paperback: 978-1-78279-476-9 ebook: 978-1-78279-475-2

Shapeshifting into Higher Consciousness
Heal and Transform Yourself and Our World with Ancient Shamanic and Modern Methods

Llyn Roberts

Ancient and modern methods that you can use every day to transform yourself and make a positive difference in the world.

Paperback: 978-1-84694-843-5 ebook: 978-1-84694-844-2

Readers of ebooks can buy or view any of these bestsellers by clicking on the live link in the title. Most titles are published in paperback and as an ebook. Paperbacks are available in traditional bookshops. Both print and ebook formats are available online.

Find more titles and sign up to our readers' newsletter at
http://www.johnhuntpublishing.com/paganism
Follow us on Facebook at
https://www.facebook.com/MoonBooks
and Twitter at https://twitter.com/MoonBooksJHP